unmasking the face

Paul Ekman is Professor of Psychology at the University of California at San Francisco. He is a fellow of the American Psychological Association and the American Association for the Advancement of Science.

Wallace V. Friesen is Lecturer in Psychology and Research Psychologist at the University of California at San Francisco, where he has worked as co-investigator with Paul Ekman since 1965.

UNMASKING THE FACE

A guide to recognizing emotions from facial clues

PAUL EKMAN and WALLACE V. FRIESEN

Consulting Psychologists Press, Inc.
577 College Ave., Palo Alto, CA 94306

For Patricia and Myriam

contents

acknowledgments *xi*

1
introduction *1*

2
**why mistakes are made
in understanding facial expressions
of emotion** *10*

3
**research on facial expressions
of emotion** *21*

4
surprise *34*

5
fear *47*

6
disgust *66*

7
anger *78*

8
happiness *99*

9
sadness *114*

10
practice faces *129*

11
facial deceit *135*

12
checking your own facial expression *154*

13
conclusion *167*

appendix I
the facial blueprint photographs *169*

appendix II
practice photos for chapter 10 *173*

appendix III
log and judge sheets *203*

index *209*

acknowledgments

We are grateful to the National Institute of Mental Health (NIMH) for making it possible for us to study facial expression and body movement during the last eighteen years. Paul Ekman was able to start our research when he was awarded a predoctoral research fellowship from NIMH from 1955 to 1957. During military service from 1958 to 1960 Ekman and Friesen became research associates, a relationship which was later formalized when Friesen joined the project in 1965. A postdoctoral research fellowship from NIMH made it possible for Ekman to pursue the research from 1960 to 1963. Later, when the pressure of teaching seemed likely to curtail research, a Career Development Award from NIMH to Ekman allowed the team to continue the research from 1966 to 1972. During all these years, at each critical juncture, the late Bert Boothe, director of the Research Fellowship Branch, provided invaluable help, interest, and advice. The Clinical Research Branch of NIMH provided continuous support for our research on facial expression and body movement from 1963 until now (MH 11976–09). Its support allowed us to study mental patients and also has made it possible for us to work together since 1965.

We are also grateful to the Advanced Research Project Agency (ARPA) of the Department of Defense for supporting our studies from 1966 to 1970. Lee Hough, former director of ARPA, convinced us of the importance of studying facial expression and gesture in different cultures. He helped us overcome our reluctance to try to resolve the argument over the possible universality of facial expression and gesture. When we launched our research in a remote area of New Guinea, Rowena Swanson, the monitor of the grant, found ways to solve the administrative and bureaucratic obstacles.

We are grateful to Silvan S. Tomkins for his contagious excitement about facial expression of emotion. He encouraged us to learn how to read faces and to teach others to do so. For the past ten years, Patsy Garlan has been an invaluable help as we have approached that point in each experiment where the results of our work are conveyed to others. She has always had a keen understanding of our research, has worked to make our writing lucid, and has critically examined our ideas and searched for ambiguities and contradictions. We are also grateful to our friends, colleagues, and employees who have been enthusiastic about our studies of the face and our attempts to teach others what we have learned. Randall Harrison, John Bear, Allen Dittmann, and Stuart Miller gave many helpful suggestions about how to present this material in an understandable way. Harriett Lukes not only typed the manuscript, but was an enthusiastic first reader. Nina Honbo helped invaluably in keeping us organized and encouraging the completion of the materials. We cannot thank by name the many people who have worked on the research reported in this book; we are grateful for their fine work and for their extra efforts which gave us the time to write this book.

Our special thanks go to our friends, students, and colleagues who let us show their faces in this book. We hope that you, our readers, get to know them well.

1

introduction

What This Book Is About

This book is about faces and feelings—your own and those of the people around you. The first focus is on what the feelings look like, in other people's faces and in your own. Photographs show the facial blueprints of the major emotions—how surprise, fear, anger, disgust, sadness, and happiness are registered by changes in the forehead, eyebrows, eyelids, cheeks, nose, lips, and chin. Common confusions that plague the recognition of expressions of emotions are clarified by pictures highlighting the differences between surprise and fear, anger and disgust, sadness and fear. The subtleties of facial expressions of emotion are revealed in pictures that show the family of expressions for each feeling. Surprise, for example, is an emotion with a big family. There is not one surprise facial expression, but many—questioning surprise, dumbfounded surprise, dazed surprise, slight, moderate, and extreme surprise. The complexities of facial expressions are shown in photographs of how different emotions can blend into a single facial expression to show sad-angry expressions, angry-afraid expressions, surprise-fearful expressions, and so forth.

You can use this information about the blueprints of facial expression to better understand the feelings of others, even when they are trying not to reveal their feelings (Chapter 11 on "Facial Deceit"). Or you can use the knowledge of the blueprints of facial expression to learn about your own face, to become more aware of what your face is telling you about how you feel and what your face is telling others. Chapter 12, "Checking Your Own Facial Expressions," describes how you can determine whether your facial expressions are characterized by a particular style. For example, are you a facial withholder (never showing anything on your face), an unwitting expressor (not knowing you are showing a feeling when you do so), or a substitute expressor (thinking you are showing an angry face when, in fact, you look sad)?

The blueprints of facial expression, whether used to understand others or yourself, is then the first focus of this book. The second focus is the feelings themselves. Although everyone uses the terms *anger, fear, sadness,* etc., few people really understand fully their own experience of these emotions. For example, what is it really like to be afraid? What does it feel like in your body? What situations make you afraid? Can you always anticipate when you will be afraid? Can you be both afraid and angry at the same time? When you are afraid, do you get aggressive, withdrawn, or thoughtful? Do you laugh fear off, or do you break out in hives? Do you ever enjoy being afraid —watching a horror movie, for example? Do other people react the same way you do when they are afraid? Does the same thing happen to their breathing? Do the same situations that make you afraid make others afraid? Or do you sometimes think or say, "I can't understand why he was afraid; that wouldn't bother me" or "I can't understand why she wasn't afraid; I was terrified."

Most people would have a difficult time answering such questions, at least about some of the emotions. This may happen when you are, to quote the cliché, out of touch with your feelings. This can also happen when you are in touch with your feelings but don't realize the extent to which your experience of an emotion is unique. There is usually one emotion, and maybe more, that you do not share openly, describing the feeling to others. It might be an emotion you in some way dread experiencing, or can't control, or habitually never think about. Or it may be an emotion you experience keenly but completely privately. You may discover, for example, after extended contact with an intimate, that what distresses you does not distress him. After the courtship is over, a marriage may founder when the mates discover they not only feel and express anger differently but that the one who explodes can't tolerate the one who holds it in, or the one with the long fuse can't accept the one with the short fuse.

The second focus of the book is upon just these issues, describing in detail the *experience* of each of the emotions. It provides as much as we know about how these emotions can be experienced in daily life. You can use this information to learn about your own emotional experiences, the things you share with others and the way in which you differ. You may find out about experiences you are missing. And you may discover the basis for some of your feelings which you have never fully understood. You can use this information also to understand other people's feelings, to have a basis other than your own emotional experience for comprehending what an emotion may be like for another human being.

Who This Book Is For

this book is for psychotherapists, ministers, physicians and nurses,
trial lawyers, personnel managers, salesmen, teachers, actors. . . .

The *psychotherapist* must know how people experience emotions. He must be alert to what the face may tell him about his patient's feelings. He can't rely solely upon the patient's words, for sometimes the patient can't describe his feelings. The patient's face may show the emotion being experienced even when it is too upsetting to put into words, when he doesn't have the words to describe his feelings, or when he doesn't know how he feels.

The *minister,* or indeed anyone who counsels people, has the same needs as the psychotherapist.

The *physician* and the *nurse* also need to understand emotions and facial expressions. People have an emotional reaction to their illness or the threat of illness which may be crucial in its outcome. The physician and the nurse must understand the different ways people experience fear, for this is a common emotional reaction to the possibility of illness and treatment, and may heighten pain, prevent early detection of illness, interfere with treatment plans, etc. And not everyone who is afraid of cancer, or surgery, will experience that fear in the same way. Recognizing sadness, which is often a reaction to loss, and helping a patient to deal with it can be an important factor in the patient's recovery when there is lingering or permanent disability. If many of the theories about psychosomatic disorder are correct, then the experience of anger also should be understood. Patients with a physical illness are often reluctant or embarrassed to mention their feelings about being sick, their fear or sadness, their feelings of self-disgust, and so forth. Physicians and nurses must, therefore, learn to interpret accurately facial expressions and facial signs that emotions are being controlled.

The *trial lawyer* often can't trust the words of a witness or client. He needs another source, such as the face, to tell him how the person really feels. Trial lawyers emphasize the importance of reading emotional reactions in picking jurors and in assessing how a jury, once selected, reacts to different lines of argument.

The *personnel manager* and the *salesman* may be in the same spot as the trial lawyer. In conducting an employment interview, the personnel manager wants to recognize signs that the applicant is controlling his feelings. For example, is his apparent confidence genuine, or is it covering nervousness about his capability. Is he really as interested in this job as he says he is. The face can allow him to check on how the applicant really feels about the job. The salesman knows that the feelings which motivate a decision to buy may never be put into words, or the words may not be trustworthy.

The *teacher* needs to know whether or not the students understand what he is saying. Interest, concentration, and perplexity are shown on the face.

The *actor* must understand the complexity of emotional experience in attempting to convey an emotion in performance. The discussion of deception may help him prevent his personal feelings from leaking through in his performance. When the actor is feeling his way into the emotional experience of a character, he needs to be sure that his expression of that emotion is commonly understood. And he should find the facial blueprints useful in understanding and perfecting his own ability to show emotions.

All these professionals—psychotherapists, physicians, nurses, trial lawyers, personnel managers, salesmen, teachers—need also to become aware, like the actor, of the impressions they give in their own facial expressions to their various "audiences."

> **this book is also for job applicants, loan seekers, customers, voters, jurymen. . . .**

The *job applicant* and the *loan seeker* need to know what impression they give by their own facial expressions to the personnel manager or bank officer, for certainly they are under scrutiny. They may want also to watch the face of the personnel manager or bank officer to gauge his reaction to them.

Customers may be concerned about the honesty of the salesman—has that car really been driven by just one little old lady?

The *voter* is often concerned with the man as well as his politics—how trustworthy he is in what he says, whether or not his campaign promises can be believed. In these days of television politics, this becomes even more of an issue.

The *juryman* can't assume that the witness or defendant is telling the truth, or knows the truth. Understanding facial expressions may help him distinguish what the person testifying actually feels from what he wants people to think he feels. The juryman must also understand the experience of emotions if he is to comprehend fully the motivations behind certain criminal acts. Whether or not there were mitigating circumstances may depend upon the emotional state of the defendant. The reliability of a witness's account may depend upon understanding his emotional experience at the time of the crime as well as at the time he is giving his account.

> **this book is for friends, spouses, parents, lovers, relatives. . . .**

The information in this book is relevant as well to any relationships that are not mechanical, perfunctory, and businesslike. Everyone has relationships in which there is little or no emotional investment. Feelings are not shared; neither person makes an attempt to know the other's feelings, and to do so would be an affront. Everyone also has relationships in which the intimate sharing of feelings is the main core. It is no accident that in intimacy faces move closer together. Intimates also look more into each others' faces. People keep in sight pictures of the faces of those with whom they feel intimate. Though a telephone call is better than a letter, if you expect an important emotional experience or want to describe one that has just occurred (wedding, divorce, death, job promotion, etc.), you want to see the look on the other person's face and you want your face to be seen.

Wanting to share feelings does not necessarily make this an easy thing to do. Intimates may find it hard to understand or accept the differences in how they experience an emotion. Intimacy may not survive such differences precisely because they are not understood. "You can't be angry about *that;* I don't believe it!" "If you were afraid, why didn't you tell me?" It is very hard to understand that people you care about, people you love, don't experience feelings the same way you do. Facial expressions that show feelings may be misinterpreted or missed entirely. If you don't fully understand the different ways a feeling may be experienced, how another's way may differ from your way of experiencing that feeling—if you don't know the various ways the face may show that same feeling—the chances for misunderstanding, for seeming inconsideration, multiply. This book is no panacea for the problems of intimacy, for not all those problems are due to misunderstanding, and misunderstandings can't be resolved by reading a book. But the descriptions of the varieties of emotional experience and the blueprints of facial expressions should help.

this book is for you alone

Understanding emotional experience applies not just to your relationships with others but also to your relationship with yourself. It can help you understand the most private, personal, unique part of your self. This is a part of your self which has enormous power over your life. Your work, your life, and even your death can be determined by your feelings. Sexual needs may not be satisfied, hunger not met, work not completed because of feelings that interfere. Feelings can motivate the taking of your own life or the life of another. Struggles of an extraordinary nature may be endured, awesome feats accomplished because of feelings. Yet we know less about our feelings than we do about our teeth, our car, or our neighbor's escapades.

This is not a self-help book, but it may lead you to a better understanding of emotions and of your own emotional life. Although learning the facial blueprints will chiefly improve your ability to spot emotion in others, it can also teach you to be keenly aware of what your own facial muscles are telling you—about you.

You can read this book, or you can study it. It depends upon your goal. Do you want simply to increase your knowledge of emotion? Or do you also want to master a skill? Both are possible, but the skills take longer to acquire than the knowledge. You can read this book in a matter of hours, concentrating on the words and looking at the pictures. You will learn a good deal about emotional experiences, your own and other people's—information that should be helpful in all the ways described above. But this approach won't teach you how to spot emotion in people's faces much better than you are already able to do. You won't be any better in spotting slight signs of emotion, blends of emotions, signs of emotional control, the leakage of emotions, and so forth. To be able to do these things requires the extra investment of learning the facial blueprints so well that you can use the information without thinking about it. It must become a skill.

You may feel you don't need much improvement in interpreting faces, or you may need it for certain emotions but not for others, or you may find you are pretty far off in telling how people feel from their faces. In the sections on facial appearance in Chapters 4, 5, 6, 7, 8, and 9 are practice instructions. Each of those chapters also tells you how to make certain faces, constructing changes in expression so you can better learn how the face works. When you can accurately recognize the faces shown in Chapters 4 through 9, Chapter 10 shows you how to use a new set of faces to practice further and improve your skills.

There is little overlap in information between this book and the popular books about body movement or nonverbal communication which have appeared in the last few years. Those books said almost nothing about facial expression, chiefly because the information about the face has not been available before. Our two previous books on facial expression (*Emotion in the Human Face* and *Darwin and Facial Expression*) are intended for the researcher who is seeking information on how to study facial expression, and for the scholar or student who wants to know what research has been done on facial expression. They address such questions as whether facial expressions of emotion are universal, and whether people can accurately tell an emotion from the face. But they don't show what universal expressions of emotion look like or show the reader how to make accurate judgments of emotion. This is our first attempt to provide this information, and to our knowledge it is the first attempt anyone has made to do this.

This book differs from the popular nonverbal-communication books, too, in that it is about the face, and therefore about emotions, while those books are primarily about the body. Our studies of the body, published in professional journals, have explored the differences in what the face and the body tell us. Emotions are shown primarily in the face, not in the body. The body instead shows how people are *coping* with emotion. There is no specific body movement pattern that always signals anger or fear, but there are facial patterns specific to each emotion. If someone is angry, his body may show how he is coping with the anger. He may be tense and constrained (tight muscular tension in arms and legs, stiff posture). He may be withdrawing (a particular retreated position). There may be verbal attack (certain types of hand movements with his words), or the likelihood of physical attack (posture, orientation, hand movements). However, any of these movements can occur just as well when a person is afraid as when he is angry. Body movement reveals, of course, not just how someone copes with emotion, but also what a person's attitudes, interpersonal orientations, etc., might be. Some of this has been explained in the popular "body" books, some has regrettably been explained badly or erroneously, and much has just not been discussed. In a few years we plan to publish another book showing how body movement, facial expression, voice tone, and words fit together. They are all important in understanding people. But the face is the key for understanding people's *emotional* expression, and it is sufficiently important, complicated, and subtle to require a book to itself.

Why There Is Need for a Book about Facial Expression

Although everyone agrees that understanding emotions is crucial to personal well-being, to intimate relationships, and to success in many professions, no one teaches you how to do this unless you get into serious trouble. And then, the various techniques of psychotherapy usually focus only on those few emotions which their theories consider. Though there is strong evidence now that the face is the primary signal system for showing the emotions, no one taught you how to read those signals. And there is every reason to believe that you were not born with the knowledge. You have to pick it up.

Much of what you know about emotions and facial expressions was shaped by your parents and other members of your family. The faces of your parents, of your siblings, and of other people who took care of you were the first you saw. Your family members may have been very expressive or very guarded in their facial expression. They may have shown you the full repertoire of emotional expressions, or only a few. Perhaps you never saw an angry face, or a fearful face. People in your family may have shown emotion in their faces as most other people do, or one of them might have developed a strange or peculiar way of looking disgusted or afraid, and that may still influence your recognition of that emotion. As a child, you may have been specifically instructed not to look at the facial expressions of others, or at least certain facial expressions. For example, some children are told never to look at someone who is crying.

As an adult, you may be more sensitive to some emotions than to others. What you learned about reading emotions in your own family might have great applicability to understanding others or relatively little, at least for some emotions. Through watching television, or movies, or a close friend, you may have improved upon and added to your knowledge of facial expressions. Although almost everyone correctly reads some facial expressions, few people realize when they make mistakes or why they make them.

The rules for translating a particular set of facial wrinkles into the judgment that a person is angry, afraid, etc. would be very hard for most people to describe. When you follow these rules you do so automatically, on the basis of habits established so long ago that usually you don't know how they operate, or even when they operate. In this sense, understanding facial expressions of emotion is like driving a car. You don't think about what you are doing when you do it. Unlike driving a car, with facial expression there never was an earlier period in which you were specifically taught the skills. There is no manual in which you can check how to correct mistakes. There are no equivalents to the traffic cop telling you when you missed or misinterpreted a signal.

Often you do not know that a facial expression was the basis for your hunch or intuition about someone. You may only sense something about a person without being able to trace the source of your impression. And if you don't know what led to your judgment you can't correct yourself if it turns out to have been wrong. Sometimes you are puzzled by someone's facial expression; you can't figure out what he meant. Or you can figure out what he meant by the look on his face, but you can't decide whether or not to trust it. It is hard to check impressions with others, because there just isn't much of a vocabulary for describing the face itself. There are a lot of words for the messages you get from the face (*afraid, terrified, horrified, apprehensive, worried,* to mention a few of those related to fear), but few to describe the source of those messages. We do have the terms *smile, grin, frown, squint,* but there are relatively few such words that identify particular facial configurations, distinctive wrinkle patterns, or temporary shapes of the facial features. Without terms to refer to the face, we are handicapped in comparing or correcting our interpretations of facial expression. Comments such as the following, though accurate, are maddeningly cumbersome. "I know why you thought he was afraid. It was because the inner corners of his eyebrows were pulled together and raised. But you failed to see the omega wrinkle in his forehead. If you had noted that, or the fact that the outer eyebrow corners were down, not up, you would have known he was sad." At best, it is not easy to describe facial expression. Pictures are needed, because it is a visual phenomenon. In this book we are able to bring you hundreds of carefully selected photographs which show you how the face registers emotion. We think such a book is needed to accomplish the following:

—Bring attention to what you may already be doing without knowing it

—Show what you may be missing entirely

—Correct what you may be misinterpreting

—Show the subtleties (the families of facial expressions) and the complexities (the blends of two emotions in one facial expression)

—Alert you to signs of facial control and teach you how to discover when a facial qualifier is used, or when an expression is modulated or falsified

—Provide techniques for learning whether you show emotion in your own face in an unusual fashion

The next chapter explains a number of the potential problems encountered in understanding facial expression, suggesting why mistakes are made and how to avoid them. You may have been brought up not to look at faces, or at certain faces. You may be distracted by other competing bids for your attention, the words someone speaks, the sound of his voice, the general appearance and movements of his body. You may not recognize the differences between controlled and uncontrolled expressions. You may not know what to look for in the face, or where to look, to tell if someone is angry, or afraid. You may not know exactly what an emotion is, how one emotion differs from another, or how an emotion differs from a mood, attitude, or character trait.

2

why mistakes are made in understanding facial expressions of emotion

The Face as a Multisignal, Multimessage System

The face provides more than one kind of signal to convey more than one kind of message. In trying to follow the emotion messages, you may look at the wrong signal. Or perhaps you don't clearly differentiate the emotion messages from the other messages conveyed by the face. A very familiar example of a multisignal, multimessage system is the system of road signs. It employs three types of signals: shape (triangular, square, circular, rectangular, octagonal), color (red, yellow, blue, green), and inscription (words, drawings, numbers). Road signs utilize these three types of signals to transmit three types of messages: regulations (stop, no U-turn, yield, etc.), warnings (school crossing, two-way traffic, etc.), and information (service area, bike route, camping, etc.). With road signs, as with facial expressions, you must focus on a particular type of signal if you wish to learn a particular type of message. If you want to know if you are approaching a rest area or a place to camp, you can search for the blue or green signs, because it is these colors that give this type of information (yellow signs give warnings, red signs give regulations). The parallel in reading faces is that if you want to know what emotion someone is feeling, you must watch the temporary changes in the face, because it is these rapid facial signals which give information about emotions. (If you were trying to determine someone's age, you would pay attention to more enduring aspects of the face, such as muscle tone or permanent wrinkles.)

The face provides three types of signals: static (such as skin color), slow (such as permanent wrinkles), and rapid (such as raising the eyebrows). The *static* signals include many more or less permanent aspects of the face—skin pigmentation, the shape of the face, bone structure, cartilage, fatty deposits, and the size, shape, and location of the facial features (brows, eyes, nose, mouth). The *slow* signals include changes in the facial appearance which occur gradually with time. In addition to the development of permanent wrinkles, changes in muscle tone, skin texture, and even skin coloration occur with age, primarily in the later years of adulthood. The *rapid* signals are produced by the movements of the facial muscles, resulting in temporary changes in facial appearance, shifts in the location and shape of the facial features, and temporary wrinkles. These changes flash on the face for a matter of seconds or fractions of a second.

All three types of facial signals can be modified or disguised by personal choice, although it is hardest to modify the static and slow signals. Hair styles are used almost universally to modify these signals. Bangs, for example, can change the apparent size of the forehead, or conceal permanently etched wrinkles. Cosmetics, such facial ornaments as sunglasses and, at the most extreme, plastic surgery can modify the static and slow facial signals so that they broadcast a different set of messages. The rapid facial signals can be modified or disguised by inhibiting the muscle movements that produce them or by masking one expression with another, or by hiding the face with beards or sunglasses. Thus, one can be misled, purposefully or accidentally, by rapid, slow, or static signals.

The face is not just a multisignal system (rapid, slow, static) but also a multimessage system. The face broadcasts messages about emotion, mood, attitudes, character, intelligence, attractiveness, age, sex, race, and probably other matters as well. This book is focused primarily on one type of message and one type of signal—emotion messages transmitted by the rapid signals. When we speak of emotions, we are referring to transitory feelings, such as fear, anger, surprise, etc. When these feelings occur, the facial muscles contract and there are visible changes in the appearance of the face. Wrinkles appear and disappear, the location and/or shape of the eyebrows, eyes, eyelids, nostrils, lips, cheeks, and chin temporarily change. Research has shown that accurate judgments of emotion can be made from the rapid facial signals, and has recently uncovered the particular facial signals—the blueprints—which distinguish each of the primary emotions. Photographs were specially made for this book to reveal and contrast the facial blueprints that distinguish each of the primary emotions and the blends of these emotions.

It is important to note that the emotion messages are not transmitted by either the slow or the static facial signals; however, these may affect the implications of an emotion message. If a person has a thin or fat face, a wrinkled or smooth face, a thin- or thick-lipped face, an old or young face, a male or female face, a Black, Oriental, or Caucasian face, that does not tell you whether the person is happy or angry or sad. But it may affect your impression. For example, if the rapid facial signals tell you that a person is angry, your impression of why the person is angry and what he is likely to do while angry may depend in part upon the information you glean from the slow and static facial signals about the person's age, sex, race, personality, temperament, and character. These further interpretations are not discussed in this book because too little is yet known about them, and because there is a prior question with which we are primarily concerned here. Before considering the matter of what you may expect of different types of people once you do know how they feel, there is the question which is the focus of this book: How do you tell from the face how someone feels, and how can you tell if his facial expression is genuine or phony?

This book also provides some information about the mood messages. Moods are closely related to emotions, and some are shown in the rapid facial signals. Moods differ from emotions in that the feelings involved last over a longer period. For example, a feeling of anger lasting for just a few minutes, or even for an hour, is called an emotion. But if the person remains angry all day, or becomes angry a dozen times during that day, or is angry for days, then it is a mood. "Irritable" is a word used to describe someone in such a mood, although one could just as well say that the person is in an angry mood. It is possible, although not likely, that a person in such a mood will show a complete anger facial expression, with the signals of anger registered over the entire face, throughout the period that the mood endures. More often just a trace of that angry facial expression may be held over a considerable period—a tightened jaw or tensed lower eyelid, or lip pressed against lip, or brows drawn down and together. Another way a mood may be registered in facial expression is by the frequency with which the total facial expression flashes on and off within some time period. It may be obvious that a person is in an irritable mood because he became angry so often this afternoon. Other moods that are shown in rapid facial expressions are depression (where the face shows evidence of sadness, fear, or a blend of both), anxiety (where the face shows evidence of fear), and euphoria (where the face shows evidence of happiness and excitement).

The rapid facial signals also send *emblematic* messages. In our research we utilize the term *emblem* to describe signals the meaning of which is very specific, the nonverbal equivalent of a common word or phrase. The eyewink signal for the message of agreement ("right on," "sure") or flirtation ("will you?") is an example. Facial emblems are like hand movements for waving "hello" or "goodbye," and like head nods for "yes" and "no." The movement is always specific and easy to distinguish from other movements. The meaning is understood by everyone in a culture or subculture. We will not discuss the full array of facial emblems, but only those which are closely related, either in movement or message, to the emotional expressions. Raising the brows and holding them while keeping the rest of the face blank is an example of such an emblem. That brow movement is part of the rapid facial signal for surprise, but when it is not joined by a movement in the eyelids and lower face as well, it signals questioning.

There are still other emblems that might be called emotion emblems, because the message they convey is about an emotion. These emotion emblems look like a facial expression of emotion, but they are different enough for the person seeing them to know that the person making them doesn't feel that way at the moment; he is just mentioning the emotion. For example, one of the emotion emblems for disgust is to wrinkle the nose, which is *part* of the disgust facial expression. When it is used as an emotion emblem it occurs alone, with little raising of the upper lip, and it flashes on and off the face quickly, and it is therefore not confused with an actual disgust facial expression. The message is "disgust (I don't feel that way now)."

The rapid facial signals are used, then, to convey emotion messages and emblematic messages. They are also used as conversational *punctuators*. Everyone knows people who use their hands to accent or italicize a word or phrase as they speak. People can do the same thing with the rapid facial signals, punctuating what is being said in words with facial accents, commas and periods. The facial punctuators will be discussed and shown in later chapters.

The face sends many rapid signals in addition to the ones that register emotion or are used in emotion-related emblems or as punctuators. Facial grimacing, contorting, and pantomiming; movements required by speech; such facial acts as lip-biting, lip-wiping, etc., will not be considered, because they are not related to or often confused with the facial expressions of emotion. Similarly, the face sends many messages in addition to those about emotions and moods. People believe they can read attitudes, personality, moral character, and intelligence from the face. We will not discuss these, because it is not known whether people even agree about such judgments, or, if so, whether their judgments are correct. Further, it is not known whether any such judgments are based on the rapid, the slow, or the static facial signals. People probably do agree and are correct, at least some of the time, in judging sex, age, and race from the face. Even with these more obvious messages, not much is known about the precise facial blueprints. Though we assume that they are transmitted primarily by the slow and static facial signals, we do not know precisely what signals transmit these types of information. For example, in reading whether someone is male or female, is this apparent in the shape of the upper or lower lip, or in the size of the lips, or the relative size of the two lips, or the pigmentation of the lips? Or is it not the lips at all, but the amount of hair in the eyebrows, or their shape; or is it the shape of the chin; etc.?

In regard to facial expressions of emotion, however, we know a good deal. We know that people can make correct judgments. We know the specific signals in each part of the face that convey the messages of fear, surprise, sadness, happiness, anger, disgust, and combinations thereof. If your understanding of facial expressions is to be improved so that you can interpret those shown by others and more adequately sense your own, then your attention must be focused upon the rapid facial signals and their distinctive messages. It is futile to look to the slow and static facial signals for information about emotion. You will need to learn the subtle and obvious differences and similarities among the emotions in their appearance on the face and in how they are experienced. And you will need to learn to distinguish the facial expressions of emotion from the facial emotion emblems, other facial emblems, and facial punctuators.

Not Watching Faces

Problems in understanding facial expressions arise because most of the time people do not watch each other's faces. Because most facial expressions of emotion are brief, you may often miss an important message. Some facial expressions are extremely rapid, lasting only a fraction of a second. We call these *micro-expressions*. Most people fail to see them or fail to recognize their importance. Later (Chapter 11) we will explain how these very quick micro-expressions can reveal emotions the person is attempting to conceal. Even the more usual macro-expressions frequently last only a few seconds. It is rare for a facial expression of emotion to last as long as five or ten seconds. If it does, the feeling must be intense, so intense that the feeling is likely to be simultaneously shown in the voice through a cry, laugh, roar, or in words. Even if you were not looking at a person's face, you would be likely not to miss these intense emotions, because you would hear them. More often, however, the very long facial expressions are not genuine expressions of emotion, but *mock* expressions, in which the person is playing at showing an emotion in an exaggerated fashion. It is obvious when you see it that the person is playing. Sometimes he may not be playing, but using the mock expression as a way to show the emotion without taking responsibility for doing so. For example, suppose you have agreed to join someone in an escapade that now, as you approach it, looks more risky than you had anticipated. You might show a mock fear expression. This would let you show how you feel, get the message across to your companion, so that he too could express hesitation; but if he is unsympathetic, he can't ridicule you because you were showing only mock fear.

It is easy to understand why the micro-expressions might be missed, because they are so quick. Later we will give some exercises for recognizing them. But even the longer macro-expressions, which last two or three seconds, are often missed, because the face is often not watched. In a sense this is paradoxical, because the face is very commanding of attention. As the site for the major sensory inputs—sight, hearing, smell, and taste—and for the major communicative output—speech—it has great importance in social life. Moreover, most people identify their very selves, in part, with their facial appearance. Industries exist around enhancing the appearance of the face. A person is most easily identified by his face, more so than by his body. His privacy is exposed much more if a picture taken of his face at some embarrassing moment appears in a newspaper, than if a similar picture of his body were to be published. And there is curiosity about other people's faces. When told about a person you haven't met, you will want to see a picture of his face; you don't usually think about wanting to see a picture that would clearly show his body. When you see a person's full face and body, you tend to look more at the face than at the body, unless perhaps there is some sexual interest.

When you converse, you seldom look continuously at the other person's face. You probably spend more time looking away from the person you are talking with than you spend looking at him. Think about how the chairs are arranged, or how you rearrange them, when you are about to sit down and have a conversation. Usually you don't sit facing each other, head-on, but adjacent to or at angles to each other. When your head is aligned with your body, you and the person you are talking with are each looking off into space, which is what you probably do most of the time. In order to see the face of the other person you must turn your head, which you will do occasionally.

Research is presently being carried on to explore just *when* two people conversing do look at each other. It seems that when you speak you look to see if the listener agrees, or is amused, angry, interested, bored, etc. You look to determine if the other person needs a chance to get a word in. You look if the other person has not made any audible listener responses for a while ("mm-hmm," "yes," "good," "uh-huh," 'is that so," etc.) to check him out. You look to give the other person the chance to take the floor. If you don't intend to give up the floor, you have to be careful not to look at the other person when you are pausing. When you are the listener, you may look at the speaker when he stresses a word, or at the end of his phrase, if his inflection rises and he seems to be inviting a verbal or nonverbal response from you.

There are some situations in which at least one person looks at the other person's face much more of the time. If you are a member of an audience, you feel no inhibition about gazing continuously at the performer's face. He has given you permission by virtue of his and your role. If you are an inter-rogator, you may continuously look at the person you are questioning; that's your job. Probably the same is true in any formal conversation in which one person has some clearly defined and acknowledged authority over another. Continuous face-watching occurs also in just the opposite type of situation. Everyone can recognize lovers, at least those who are still courting, by how much of the time they unabashedly gaze into each other's faces.

Why is it that most of the time you don't look at the face of the person you are conversing with? Why may you actually look away at just the mo-ment you sense he may show an emotional facial expression? Part of the answer is politeness—being brought up not to stare (at least in the U.S. and some other cultures). You don't want to be rude and intrusive, taking infor-mation that it is not clear the other person is giving to you. And you don't want to embarrass the person you are conversing with, or yourself. If he wants you to know how he feels, then he can say it in words; otherwise you would be overstepping the bounds of convention. Watching someone's face is intimate. You take such a liberty only if the other person gives it to you by being a public performer, or if your social role bestows it upon you (as interrogator, employer, juryman, parent, etc.)—or if you avowedly seek to share intimacy, looking and inviting the look of the other person.

There is another side to it, however. It is not just being polite and not wanting to embarrass or be embarrassed. Often not looking at the other per-son's face is motivated by not wanting to be burdened with that knowledge or obligated to do something about how the person feels. By not looking at his face you don't know, or can pretend not to know. Unless he says it in words, you are not socially obligated to care for or respond to his feelings. If he is showing annoyance or anger on his face and you see it, and he knows you see it, then you may have to find out whether you are the cause, or if not, why he is angry. If he is showing sadness, you may have to comfort or aid him; the same is true if he is showing fear. In many social interactions the last thing either person wants is to acknowledge or take any responsibility for having to deal with the feelings of the other person.

In addition to these fairly common reasons for not looking at faces, some people may have had experiences in their childhood which trained them not to look at certain people's facial expressions, or at certain expres-sions, no matter who shows them. A child may learn that it is dangerous to look at Daddy's face when he is angry, or dangerous to look at anyone's angry face. Such learning may occur so early that the grown person avoids seeing certain emotions, or certain types of people showing certain emotions, without knowing he is engaged in such avoidance.

If your understanding of facial expressions is to improve, then you must reexamine whether or when you want to know how the other person feels. You may have to counteract habits you have learned and followed without knowing it, which lead you to ignore and miss many facial expressions of emotion.

The Communication Barrage

The face is but one source of information available during a conversation, and the problem is that messages may be missed because of the distraction of the other, more commanding sources bidding for attention. In most conversations it is sight and sound, what you see and hear, that you rely upon. In most conversations among people from Western industrialized settings, there is not much tactile stimulation, and precautions are taken to camouflage odors. When listening, you gather information from at least three sources in the *auditory* channel: the actual words used; the sound of the voice; and such things as how rapidly the words are spoken, how many pauses there are, how much the speech is disrupted by words like "aah" or "ummh." When looking, you gather information from at least four sources in the *visual* channel: the face; the tilts of the head; the total body posture; and the skeletal muscle movements of the arms, hands, legs, and feet. Every one of these sources in both the auditory and visual channel can tell you something about emotion.

The auditory and visual channels offer different advantages and disadvantages in communication to the sender and receiver of messages. The auditory channel can be completely turned off by the sender; he can simply shut up and thereby cease providing any information to the other person he was conversing with. This is an advantage for the sender, a disadvantage to the receiver. The visual channel is in some sense always turned on. The sender must maintain some body posture, some hand position, some set to the face; thus, some impression is always given to the other person.

If the sender can assume that the other person is interested in the conversation, the use of the auditory channel provides greater likelihood that a message sent will get through and be received. The listener does not need to point his ears at the sender to receive a message; the listener's auditory channel is open. Not so with the visual channel. The other person might be interested, but fail to glance over at the moment a message is sent. The sender may take advantage of this to "slot" a message in the visual channel to comment to an onlooker without the knowledge of the person with whom he is conversing. For example, one person may signal visually to another person to rescue him from a boring conversation, without the boring conversant noticing the call for help. On the other hand, if the sender does want his message to get through to the other person with whom he is conversing, then he must wait until the other person is visually fixed on him before sending a message in the visual channel. Thus, when a sender and receiver share an interest in communicating, the auditory channel has the advantage of more certain receipt of messages sent.

On the other hand, the receiver can more easily pretend auditory than visual interest. Listening can be simulated, with occasional nods and "um-hmms" thrown in, when in fact the receiver is listening to another conversation or to his own thoughts. There are no tell-tale signs of such auditory disloyalty which parallel the out-of-focus look to the gaze, if the viewer pretends to be looking at the sender but is in fact looking at someone behind or to the side of him; nothing to equal the tracking movements which show that the viewer's eyes are following someone else's activity. Incidentally, because it is more obvious who is looking than who is listening, both sender and receiver have more protection from eavesdropping by unwanted lookers than by unwanted listeners.

Although there is some repetition or overlap in the type of information transmitted in the two channels, there is a natural division of labor, so that each channel better conveys certain messages. Words are best for most messages, particularly factual ones. If you are trying to tell someone where the museum is, who played the lead in that movie, whether you are hungry, or how much the meal costs, you use words. You don't resort to the visual channel as the primary transmitter of such messages unless you can't speak or be heard, or unless the message involves showing where something is in space (how you get to the post office from here). The voice tone and the visual channel sources add qualifying messages to what is transmitted in words. Nuances are added, points emphasized, instructions given as to how seriously to take what is said in words, etc. The visual channel also can be used for factual messages, by Indian sign language or the language of the deaf, but the advantage is clearly with words.

Words can also be used to describe feelings or explain them, and typically are used in concert with other sources to do so. Here, however, the advantage is with the visual channel, because the rapid facial signals are the primary system for expression of emotions. It is the face you search to know whether someone is angry, disgusted, afraid, sad, etc. Words cannot always describe the feelings people have; often words are not adequate to express what you see in the look on someone's face at an emotional moment. And words are not trusted as much as faces, when it comes to emotions. If someone tells you he is angry and his face shows it as well, nothing is amiss. But if he says he is angry and shows no evidence facially, you are suspicious. If the reverse occurs and he looks angry but doesn't mention anger feelings in his words, you doubt the words but not the anger; you wonder why he doesn't admit how he feels.

Emotion messages can also be transmitted by the sound of the voice, body posture, hand/arm movements, and leg/feet movements. But it is not certain whether they transmit information about emotion with as much precision as does the face. They may more simply tell you that someone is upset, but not whether the upset feeling is anger, fear, disgust, or sadness. The clarity and precision of these other sources of emotion messages remains to be studied. We do know that the face is a primary, clear, and precise signal system for the expression of the specific emotions.

With two channels—the auditory and visual—transmitting information from seven sources, communication is a barrage. The speaker sends out a barrage of signals and may not carefully attend to or employ all of them in an optimal fashion, and the listener is barraged and may not attend to all the signals available. With the visual channel, people focus more on the face than on the other sources; facial expressions are tuned more than body movements, and people look at faces more than body movements. But the auditory channel, in particular the words, usually receives the most attention, both from speaker and listener, because here can be transmitted the richest and most varied information about everything but emotion.

You can miss important information about emotions in the face, then, because it is competing with these other information sources, and it may be somewhat handicapped in its bid for attention. Even if you focused as much on facial expressions as on words, the words would receive more attention because they always reach us, while one has to look to see a facial expression. The face is, nevertheless, of more importance than words for transmitting information about emotion.

Controlling the Face

Facial expression may be controlled or uncontrolled. One expression may be voluntary, another involuntary; one may be truthful and another false. The problem is to tell which is which.

Suppose someone has an emotional experience—something happens, let us say, to make him afraid. If an expression of fear comes over his face, it will have done so automatically. The person does not think about how to move his facial muscles to look afraid; the fear expression is involuntary. But there may be interference, dictated either by longstanding well-ingrained habit or by deliberate, self-conscious choice of the moment. The interference may be minor, only qualifying or modulating the expression, or major, interrupting or totally inhibiting the expression. The facial expression of fear would be qualified if the person added to the fear expression a bit of a smile, showing that he can "grin and bear it." The facial expression would be modulated if the person changed the apparent intensity of the expression, trying to show only slight worry when experiencing strong fear. The facial expression of fear could be interrupted, so that only a trace appeared; or the expression might be totally inhibited so that nothing showed on the face, or there was only a stiff appearance. Not only can facial expressions be interfered with, but people can simulate emotion expressions, attempting to create the impression that they feel an emotion when they are not experiencing it at all. A person may show an expression that looks like fear when in fact he feels nothing, or feels sadness or some other emotion.

Facial expressions of emotion are controlled for various reasons. There are social conventions about what you can show on your face, cultural display rules that govern how people manage the appearance of their faces in public. For example, in the United States many little boys learn the cultural display rule, "little men do not cry or look afraid." There are also more personal display rules, not learned by most people within a culture, but the product of the idiosyncrasies of a particular family. A child may be taught never to look angrily at his father, or never to show sadness when disappointed, or whatever. These display rules, whether cultural ones shared by most people or personal, individual ones, are usually so well-learned, and learned so early, that the control of the facial expression they dictate is done automatically without thinking or awareness.

Facial expressions are also controlled because of vocational need or practice. Some jobs seem to require or select people who are expert facial controllers. Anyone who is successful in such a job may need to be able to put on convincing simulations (the actor, or even the salesman). Or the requirement may be never to reveal how you actually feel (the diplomat). People also control their facial expressions of emotion because it is to their advantage at a particular moment. If a pupil cheats on an exam, he may conceal his apprehension when the proctor walks by because he doesn't want to get caught.

Some of the confusion about facial expression arises, then, because the face conveys both true and false emotion messages. There are uncontrolled, involuntary, true expressions and also qualified, modulated, or false expressions, with lies of omission through inhibition and lies of commission through simulation. In order to improve your understanding of facial expressions of emotion, you will have to distinguish which is which. The first step is to learn how the actually felt emotions appear on the face (Chapters 4 to 9), for without that knowledge you can't spot the clues to facial control. Later, in Chapter 11 on "Facial Deceit," the display rules and the various management techniques will be further explained. A number of suggestions will be given about how to distinguish felt from modulated or false facial expressions. Some of the clues are in the shape of the facial expression, some in its timing, others in its location in the conversational stream, and still others in how the facial expression relates to everything else the person is doing.

3

research on facial expressions
of emotion

There have been hundreds of experiments on facial expressions of emotion. Elsewhere we have analyzed these studies in detail (see Reference 5 at the end of this chapter). Here we will more briefly describe only those studies which are directly relevant to the information presented in this book. This chapter should help resolve the doubts of the skeptic about the scientific basis for what is said and shown in subsequent chapters. It is also provided for those who are curious about how facial expressions of emotion are studied.

Which Emotions Does the Face Show?

Does the face tell us only whether someone feels pleasant or unpleasant, or does it provide more precise information, conveying which unpleasant emotion is experienced? If the latter, how many of these specific emotions does the face show—six, eight, twelve, or what number? The typical method used to determine just which emotions can be read from the face has been to show photographs of facial expressions to observers, who are asked to say what emotion they see in each face. The observers may be given a predetermined list of emotion words to choose from, or left to their own resources to reply with whatever emotion word comes to mind. The investigator analyzes the answers of the different observers to determine what emotions they agree about in describing particular faces. He might find, for example, that 80 percent of the observers agree in describing a particular face with the word "afraid." They might not agree about a word to describe some other face; for example, a face called "disinterest" by some observers might be labeled with other emotions by other observers. On the basis of such results, the investigator reaches a conclusion about which emotions the face can convey.

The six emotions that are the subject of this book—happiness, sadness, surprise, fear, anger, and disgust—were found by every investigator in the last thirty years who sought to determine the vocabulary of emotion terms associated with facial expressions. There are probably other emotions conveyed by the face—shame and excitement, for example; but these have not yet been as firmly established. Because we will be showing not only how these six emotions appear on the face, but also how thirty-three different blends of these six emotions appear, quite a large portion of the emotional repertoire of the face will be represented.

Are Judgments of Emotion Accurate?

It is not enough to determine what emotions are read from facial expressions. It is also crucial to discover whether the interpretations of the observers are correct or not. When people look at someone's face and think that person is afraid, are they right or wrong? Are facial expressions an accurate reflection of emotional experience? Or are the impressions gained from facial expression merely stereotypes—all agree about them, but they are wrong? To study this question the investigator must find some people whom he knows to be having a particular emotional experience. He must take some photographs, films, or videotapes of these people and then show them to observers. If the observers' judgments of the facial expressions fit with the investigator's knowledge of the emotional experience of the persons being judged, then accuracy is established.

Most of the studies of accuracy in judging facial expression failed to provide conclusive evidence one way or another, usually because the investigator's knowledge of the emotional experience of the people being judged was faulty. In our analysis of the experiments conducted over the last fifty years, we did find consistent and conclusive evidence that accurate judgments of facial expression can be made. Some of these studies were conducted in our own laboratory. In one experiment, photographs were taken of psychiatric patients when they were admitted to a mental hospital, and again when they were less upset and ready for discharge. Untrained observers were shown these photographs and asked whether each facial expression was shown at time of admission or at time of discharge. The judgments were accurate. These same photographs were shown to another group of observers who were not told they were seeing photographs of psychiatric patients, but instead were asked to judge whether the emotion shown was pleasant or unpleasant. Again accuracy was proven, because the facial expressions shown at admission were judged as more unpleasant than those shown at discharge from the hospital. In another study, other observers were asked to judge how pleasant or unpleasant the facial expressions were, but the faces shown to them were of psychiatric trainees undergoing a stress interview. Without knowing which was which, the observers judged the facial expressions during stress as more unpleasant than the facial expressions drawn from a non-stressful part of the interview. In still another experiment, observers were shown two films of college students, one taken when they had been watching a very unpleasant film of surgery, and one when they had been watching a pleasant travelogue film. The observers accurately judged which film the college students were watching from their facial expressions.

All these studies were concerned with spontaneous facial expressions which naturally occur when a person does not deliberately try to show an emotion in his face. But what of those situations in which a person deliberately tries to show an emotion, to look happy or angry, etc.? Many studies have indicated that observers can accurately judge which emotion is intended when a person deliberately tries to convey an emotion through facial expression.

Are There Universal Facial Expressions of Emotion?

Are facial expressions of emotion the same for people everywhere, no matter what their background? When someone is angry, will we see the same expression on his face regardless of his race, culture, or language? Or are facial expressions a language, the meaning of which we must learn anew for each culture, just as we need to learn the verbal language? A little more than one hundred years ago, Charles Darwin (see Reference 1 at the end of this chapter) wrote that facial expressions of emotion are universal, not learned differently in each culture; that they are biologically determined, the product of man's evolution. Since Darwin's time many writers have emphatically disagreed. Just recently, however, scientific investigations have conclusively settled this question, showing that the facial appearance of at least some emotions, those covered in this book, is indeed universal, although there are cultural differences in when these expressions are shown.

Research conducted in our laboratory played a central role in settling the dispute over whether facial expressions are universal or specific to each culture. In one experiment, stress-inducing films were shown to college students in the United States and to college students in Japan. Part of the time, each person watched the film alone and part of the time the person watched while talking about the experience with a research assistant from the person's own culture. Measurements of the actual facial muscle movements, captured on videotapes, showed that when they were alone, the Japanese and Americans had virtually identical facial expressions (see Figure 1). When in the presence of another person, however, where cultural rules about the management of facial appearance (display rules) would be applied, there was little correspondence between Japanese and American facial expressions. The Japanese masked their facial expressions of unpleasant feelings more than did the Americans. This study was particularly important in demonstrating what about facial expression is universal and what differs for each culture. The universal feature is the distinctive appearance of the face for each of the primary emotions. But people in various cultures differ in what they have been taught about managing or controlling their facial expressions of emotion.

In another experiment we showed photographs of the different emotion expressions to observers in the United States, Japan, Chile, Argentina, and Brazil. The observers in these different cultures had to choose one of the six primary emotion words for each photograph they saw. If facial expressions were a language that differs from culture to culture, then a facial expression said to be *angry* by Americans might be called *disgust* or *fear* by people in Brazil, or might not mean anything to them. Just the opposite was found. The same facial expressions were judged as showing the same emotions in all these countries, regardless of language or culture (see Figure 2). Essentially the same experiment was carried out independently at the same

Fig. 1 Example of spontaneous facial expression of a Japanese (on the left) and an American (on the right) shown when watching a stress film.

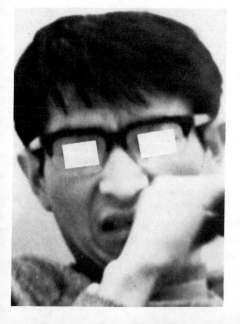 

Fig. 2 Examples of the photographs utilized in a study of how emotions are judged across literate cultures

Percentage Agreement in How Photograph Was Judged Across Cultures

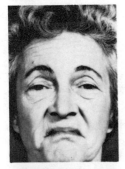

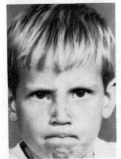

	UNITED STATES (J=99)	BRAZIL (J=40)	CHILE (J=119)	ARGEN- TINA (J=168)	JAPAN (J=29)
Fear	85%	67%	68%	54%	66%
Disgust	92%	97%	92%	92%	90%
Happiness	97%	95%	95%	98%	100%
Anger	67%	90%	94%	90%	90%

time by Carroll Izard (Reference 8) with observers in eight different cultures, and the same evidence of universality was found.

Although we wished to interpret our findings as evidence that some facial expressions are universal, one loophole remained. All the people studied had some shared visual contact, usually not directly but through the mass media. It was still possible that facial expressions might really differ in all the cultures studied, but the people might have learned, through movies, television, and picture magazines, what each other's facial expressions of emotion looked like. Or facial expressions of emotion might be similar in all the cultures we studied precisely because the people had all learned how to show emotion on their face by watching the same actors in the movies or television and imitating their facial expressions. We had not eliminated the possibility that, among people who did not have the opportunity to view mass-media portrayals of facial expressions of emotion, emotions would be shown by entirely different facial muscular movements. The only way to settle this question was to study visually isolated people who had no contact with the mass-media, and little if any contact with the outside world.

We conducted a series of experiments in the Southeast Highlands of New Guinea, where we were able to find people who met these criteria. Because these people were in no way accustomed to taking psychological tests or participating in experiments, and because we did not know their language but had to work through translators, we had to modify our experimental procedure. In other countries we had shown a single photograph of one or another of the emotion expressions and given the observer a choice among a list of emotion words. In New Guinea, we showed the person three photographs at once, had a translator read an emotion story, such as "A person's mother died," and asked the observer to point to the photograph that fit the story. We found that these people selected the same face for the same emotion as did people in all the other cultures we had studied. There was but one exception: the New Guineans failed to distinguish between the fear and surprise facial expressions.

In a related experiment, other New Guineans were told an emotion story and each was asked to show the emotion on his own face. Videotapes were taken of these intended emotion expressions, some examples of which are shown in Figure 3. Analysis of these New Guineans' facial expressions showed again that the same facial expressions were produced for the same emotions as had been found in other cultures, with the exception of fear and surprise, which were confused with each other. Further confirmation of the universality of facial expressions was obtained by a study of another culture in West Irian, the western portion of the island of New Guinea. Karl and Eleanor Heider, who were skeptical of our evidence of universality, conducted the same experiments with people even more visually isolated than those we had studied, and they also obtained evidence of universality.

Taken together, our studies, those of Izard, the Heiders' study, and evidence from Eibl-Eibesfeldt (an ethologist using very different methods), showed quite conclusively that Darwin was correct in claiming that there are universal facial expressions of emotion.

Although the appearance of the face for each of the primary emotions is common to all peoples, facial expressions do vary across cultures in at least two respects. What elicits or calls forth an emotion will usually differ; people

Fig. 3   Video frames of attempts to pose emotion by subjects from the Fore of New Guinea. The instruction for the top left photograph was "your friend has come and you are happy"; for the top right "your child has died"; for the bottom left "you are angry and about to fight"; for the bottom right "you see a dead pig that has been lying there for a long time."

may become disgusted or afraid in response to different things in different cultures. Also, cultures differ in the conventions people follow in attempting to control or manage the appearance of their faces in given social situations. People in two different cultures may feel sadness at the death of a loved one, but one culture may prescribe that the chief mourners mask their facial expression with a mildly happy countenance.

How Does Each Emotion Appear on the Face?

As we began to find evidence that there are some facial expressions of emotion which are universal, and before all the studies were completed, we began to investigate just what these universal facial expressions of emotion look like. We sought to construct an *Atlas* of the face, which would depict photographically each of the universal facial expressions of emotion. It is this Atlas (Reference 4) which forms the basis for the photographs shown in the subsequent chapters of this book. Our first step in developing the Facial Atlas was to study what others had said about the appearance of the face for each of the primary emotions. Some writers had described which muscles were contracted in particular emotions, while others concerned themselves only with the appearance of the surface of the face. None had systematically considered all the muscles or all the consequent changes in the surface appearance of the face for the six primary emotions.

Putting together what was written by Darwin, Duchenne, a French anatomist whom Darwin had quoted extensively, Huber (Reference 7), an American anatomist writing thirty years ago, and Plutchik (Reference 9), an American psychologist concerned with emotion, we saw part of the picture emerge. We constructed a table which listed all the facial muscles and the six emotions, entering into the table what these men had written about which muscles were involved in what way for each emotion. There were many gaps, however, where no one had said anything about the involvement of a particular muscle in a particular emotion. Working with Silvan Tomkins (Reference 10), we filled in those gaps with information from our cross-cultural studies and our shared impressions.

The next step was to photograph models, who were instructed to move particular facial muscles listed in the table. We separately photographed the three areas of the face which are capable of independent movement—the brow/forehead; the eyes/lids and root of the nose; and the lower face, including the cheeks, mouth, most of the nose, and chin. The completed Atlas consists of a series of photographs of these three different areas of the face, each photograph keyed to one of the six emotions. As might well be expected, for each of the emotions there is more than one Atlas photograph for at least one facial area. For example, for surprise there is one brow/forehead, one eyes/lids/root of nose, but four different Atlas photographs of the lower face.

The next obvious question was whether the Atlas is correct. Are the six emotions—happiness, sadness, anger, fear, disgust, and surprise—in actuality composed of the facial appearances listed in the Atlas? Or does the Atlas appearance of disgust actually occur with anger, and so forth? We have conducted four experiments on the validity of the Atlas. Two of the experiments attempted to prove its validity by showing that measurements of the face with the Atlas corresponded with other evidence of the subjective emotional experience of the persons whose faces were measured. These experiments investigated the experiential validity of the Atlas.

The other two experiments investigated the social validity of the Atlas. Rather than attempting to prove that the Atlas measurements correspond to the person's experience, these studies investigated whether the Atlas measurements can predict what observers think a person is feeling when they look at his face. Although experiential and social validity should be related, they need not necessarily be so. We may not look to others how we actually feel, at least all the time. Thus, it was necessary to study both experiential and social validity.

The studies of experiential validity drew from materials gathered in one of the cross-cultural studies of facial expressions described earlier. College students in Japan and in the United States had individually watched pleasant and unpleasant movies while we videotaped their facial expressions. From their answers to questionnaires after the experiment, it was clear that they experienced very different emotions while watching the two films. In describing their reactions to the travelogue, the subjects had said it was interesting and pleasant, and caused them to feel moderate happiness. In describing their reactions to the surgical film, the subjects said they had unpleasant, disgusted, pained, fearful, sad, and surprised feelings. If the Facial Atlas is valid, then measurements based on it should be able to distinguish between the facial expressions shown when these two different sets of emotions were experienced.

All the facial muscular movements visible on the videotapes were isolated, their duration was measured, and they were classified in terms of the Atlas. This measurement procedure was done in slow motion, with the measurements made separately for the three areas of the face, by three separate technicians. Such precise measurement required about five hours for each minute of videotaped facial behavior. The results were very clear-cut. Measurements with the Facial Atlas clearly distinguished the two emotional conditions—whether subjects had been watching a stressful film or a travelogue. And the Atlas was equally successful with the facial expressions of Japanese subjects and with Americans, as it should be, because it was built to show the universal facial expressions of emotion. One limitation of this experiment, however, is that it didn't determine whether the Atlas correctly depicts the facial appearances for each of the six emotions. It only shows that the Atlas is correct in distinguishing between unpleasant and pleasant experiences.

The second experiential validity study provided a partial remedy to this limitation. Recent research on the physiology of emotions suggests that there are markedly different patterns of heart rate acceleration and deceleration with the emotions of surprise and disgust. Measures of heart rate and skin conductance had been gathered on the Japanese and American subjects when they were watching the pleasant and stressful films. If the Atlas is correct in what it says a surprise face and a disgust face look like, then when the Atlas says such facial expressions occur, there should be a different pattern of heart rate for each. When we examined the changes in heart rate which coincided with facial expressions the Atlas had designated as either surprise or disgust, the results showed the predicted difference.

Although this second study does provide evidence of the validity of the Atlas for surprise and disgust, it doesn't show that the Atlas is necessarily valid in what it says about the other emotions—anger, happiness, sadness, and fear. Logically, if it is shown to be valid for surprise and disgust, the Atlas should be equally valid for the other emotions, because it was derived by the same method for all six emotions. But evidence is still required, and for that we turn to the third study, which examined the Atlas in terms of social validity. Could the Atlas predict how observers will interpret facial expressions?

Photographs that had been taken by many different investigators of facial expression were obtained. These pictures were shown to observers, who were asked to judge which of the six emotions was shown in each picture. Only those on which the observers had agreed about the emotion expressed in the face were further considered. If the Atlas correctly depicts the appearance of each of the six emotions, then measurements based on the Atlas ought to be able to predict the emotion seen by the observers in each of these photographs. The Atlas measurements were made separately for the three areas of the face by three separate technicians, and predictions were made. With great success the Atlas predicted the emotions seen by observers when they looked at each of these photographs of facial expression.

The fourth study was much like the one just described, except that here the facial expressions examined were those produced by dental and nursing students who had been instructed to attempt to show each of the six emotions by their facial expression. The problem was for the Atlas to predict for each photograph what emotion the student had been intending to show. The measurements made with the Atlas succeeded.

While we were working on these experiments, independently and unknown to us a Swedish anatomist, Carl-Herman Hjortsjö (Reference 6), was working with very different methods on the same problem. He photographed his own face as he contracted each of the facial muscles. Hjortsjö then looked at each of these photographs and asked what emotion these pictures seemed to show. On the basis of his own judgment, he then described in his Atlas the appearance of the facial expressions for each emotion. When we recently met with Hjortsjö, we were all pleased to discover that there was almost complete overlap between his Atlas and ours.

Although no one of our four experiments alone would validate the Atlas, taken together and in conjunction with the independent discovery of the same Facial Atlas by Hjortsjö, the evidence for the validity of our Atlas is much more than tentative. Much research remains to be done to further validate and refine the Atlas; but the evidence is sufficient to share what we have already found. The information presented in the subsequent chapters about the appearance of the facial expressions is based on the Atlas and has been supported by one or more of our own experiments or by Hjortsjö's work. The photographs show only part of what is in our Atlas. We have selected those parts which are best supported by evidence and which are most important for learning the practical skill of reading facial expressions of emotion. It is unlikely that anything shown is in error. But it is likely that we are only telling part of the story, that further research will determine additional ways in which the facial expressions of emotion can be shown.

How Are Facial Expressions Controlled?

How can we tell a real facial expression of emotion from a simulated one? When a person doesn't feel the way he looks, but is attempting to mislead us about his feelings, is there any way to detect his real feelings in his facial expression? In short, does the face "leak"?

We have been studying this problem for a number of years. We started with films of the facial expressions of psychiatric patients during interviews. In certain interviews we knew from subsequent events that the patients had been misleading the interviewer about their feelings. Study of these films provided the basis for a theory of nonverbal *leakage*—ways to tell, from facial expression or body movement, feelings the person was attempting to conceal. We have been testing this theory during the last few years by studying interviews in which one person purposefully conceals from another the negative emotions experienced as a result of watching very unpleasant, stress movies. The subjects in this experiment try to convince the interviewer that the film they have seen was actually pleasant, and that they enjoyed it.

Our study of these interviews is far from completed. We have yet to test many of our hypotheses about facial leakage. However, our findings to date are consistent with our hypotheses and with our earlier findings from the interviews with psychiatric patients. The information presented in Chapter

11 on "Facial Deceit" must be regarded as tentative. It is our best judgment of what the research will prove, based on our theory and our many hours of inspecting facial expressions of people when they are lying.

How Are the Emotions Experienced?

We have not directly studied this question, and had thought in planning this book that we would be able to rely upon the scientific literature. We were disappointed to find that despite many studies of emotion and a variety of theories of emotion, relatively little attention has been paid to certain fundamental questions. What, for instance, are the different events which call forth each emotion? What are the variations in the intensity of each emotion? How do the sensations for each emotion differ? And what are the likely activities people will engage in when they feel angry, disgusted, afraid, etc.?

There were some answers, or ideas about some of these matters, for some of the emotions. Of most help were the writings of Darwin and of Tomkins. Much of what we have written had to be extrapolated from our own experiences and the many years of thinking about the six emotions whose facial expressions we have been studying. In each of the next chapters is a section on "The Experience of . . ." which presents most of what has been scientifically established about each emotion, and much that has not been established scientifically, although it should be familar to everyone. A number of our friends and colleagues have checked these parts of the book and found them to fit their own lives and their knowledge of the lives of others. You will be able to determine the value of these discussions by comparing them with your own experience and that of your friends. If something that is said about anger, for example, doesn't fit your experience or that of your friends, we may be wrong. If it doesn't fit your experience, but makes sense to friends, you will have discovered a way in which your experience (or your friends') of that emotion is special.

References

For those interested in learning more about facial expression, a list of some of the most important works on this topic follows.

1. CHARLES DARWIN, *The Expression of the Emotions in Man and Animals.* London: John Murray, 1872. (Current edition: University of Chicago Press, 1965.) This is the seminal book on facial expressions, in which Darwin presented his observations on facial expressions in animals, human children, blind humans, and members of different cultures.

2. IRANEUS EIBL-EIBESFELDT, *Ethology, the Biology of Behavior.* New York: Holt, Rinehart & Winston, 1970. A leading ethologist describes his work, primarily on animals. One chapter deals with his study of facial expressions in humans in various visually isolated cultures, and presents his conclusion that facial expressions of emotion are universal.

3. PAUL EKMAN, Ed., *Darwin and Facial Expression: A Century of Research in Review.* New York: Academic Press, 1973. Separate chapters review and integrate the studies conducted over the last hundred years on facial expressions in infants and children, in nonhuman primates, and in people from different cultures. The book concludes that many of Darwin's ideas about facial expression have been supported.

4. PAUL EKMAN and WALLACE V. FRIESEN. *Facial Action Coding System.* Palo Alto: Consulting Psychologists Press, 1978. Complete atlas, including photographs and film strips, for learning to measure and score facial behavior. Designed for the serious research worker.

5. PAUL EKMAN, WALLACE V. FRIESEN, and PHOEBE ELLSWORTH, *Emotion in the Human Face.* Elmsford, New York: Pergamon Press, 1972. This critical review and integration of the quantitative research on human facial expression conducted over a fifty-five-year period presents answers to seven major research questions, suggestions for further research, and guidelines about how to conduct such research.

6. CARL-HERMAN HJORTSJÖ, *Man's Face and Mimic Language.* Studentlitteratur, Lund, Sweden, 1970. An anatomist describes the facial musculature and the particular muscular movements associated with the emotions. Drawings of the face are used to show both the muscle movements and the changed appearance of the surface of the face.

7. ERNST HUBER, *Evolution of Facial Musculature and Facial Expression.* Baltimore: The Johns Hopkins Press, 1931. An anatomist discusses the evolution of the facial musculature from the lower vertebrates through the primates. A major emphasis is on differences in the facial musculature among different genetic human groups, with some attention to emotional expression.

8. CARROLL E. IZARD, *The Face of Emotion.* New York: Appleton-Century-Crofts, 1971. This historical review of theories of emotion is a presentation of the author's own theory, based largely on the work of Silvan Tomkins, and on research across cultures and among children. Only slight attention is paid to how the emotions appear on the face.

9. ROBERT PLUTCHIK, *The Emotions.* New York: Random House, 1962. Another historical review of theories of emotion, this book presents the author's own theory and research in support of it. Only slight attention is paid to how the emotions appear on the face.

10. SILVAN S. TOMKINS, *Affect, Imagery, Consciousness,* vols. I and II. New York: Springer Publishing Co., 1962, 1963. An extraordinary, complicated, and fascinating theory that emphasizes the importance of emotion in the psychology of human behavior. Broad in its scope, this work consistently emphasizes the role of the face in human life.

4

surprise

Surprise is the briefest emotion. It is sudden in its onset. If you have time to think about the event and consider whether or not you are surprised, then you are not. You can never be surprised for long, unless the surprising event unfolds new surprising elements. It doesn't linger. When you cease being surprised, its disappearance is often as sudden as was it onset.

Surprise is triggered both by the *un*expected and by what might be called the *"mis*expected" event. Suppose a man's wife appears in his office. If she customarily comes at that time to drop off his lunch he will not be surprised. The appearance of his wife is neither unexpected nor misexpected. If his wife rarely comes to his office, but her impending visit is announced by his secretary saying, "I can see your wife coming up the street," he will not be surprised when she arrives, because there will have been time to anticipate and perhaps figure out an explanation for this out-of-the-ordinary event. If his wife walks in unannounced and it is unusual for her to appear at her husband's office, then the event is an *unexpected* surprise—an unusual event which was unanticipated. It is called *un*expected rather than *mis*-expected because at that moment the surprised person was not expecting anything in particular to happen. If, however, the coffee vendor always comes by at that time and always gives a characteristic knock on the door, and it is the man's wife, not the coffee vendor who comes in, the event is a *mis*-expected surprise. There was an aroused specific anticipation for something different to happen at that moment. In misexpected surprise the event need not be unusual to be surprising; it is the contrast with what is expected at that moment that is surprising. If, at the moment that the coffee vendor was expected, the secretary came in, there still might be surprise, probably slight surprise. If, in addition, the event that is contrary to what is expected is also unusual, then the surprise will be greater. The wife at that moment would be more surprising than the secretary.

Almost anything can be surprising, provided it is either unexpected or misexpected. A sight, sound, smell, taste, or touch can be surprising. When one bites into a pastry that looks as if it is filled with chocolate cream, the taste of savory pork and mushrooms can be a surprise. The taste was misexpected. Not only physical sensations trigger surprise. An unanticipated or misanticipated idea, comment, or suggestion of another person can be surprising. So can a novel thought or feeling of your own. The technique of many mystery stories is not just to make the reader afraid (that is the ghost or horror-story genre), but also to surprise the reader with whodunnit. Many jokes rely upon misexpectation to achieve their humor. Your amusement depends upon being taken in by the plot of the joke, and surprised by the twist ending.

If you have time to anticipate an event and do so correctly, then you cannot be surprised. If the man in our example could have seen his wife approach his office, he might have been surprised at his first sight of her, but by the time his wife knocked on his door—no surprise. Or if he had known his wife was going to be near his office shopping that morning, no surprise. Surprise lasts only until you have evaluated just what it was that occurred. Once you have determined the nature of the surprising event, you are no longer surprised. Usually there is a ready explanation—"I was shopping, ran out of checks, came by to get some blank checks from you, met the coffee vendor in the hallway, and got your coffee from him." If the event resists interpretation, the surprise lingers; you may become disoriented, fearful, or mystified. Suppose a woman is greeted on the doorstep by the husband whom she had thought was killed in the war. Surprise. But it ends when he explains, "I'm your husband's twin brother." or "I was missing in action, and had amnesia." If the interpretation is even more unlikely than the event, she may be surprised all over again, fearful or mystified—"I'm the spirit of your husband returned to talk to you."

Once you have evaluated the unexpected or misexpected event, you move quickly from surprise into another emotion. "What a happy surprise," you say, not realizing that surprise itself is neutral in hedonic tone. It is, rather, the following emotion that gives a positive or negative tone to the experience, depending upon the nature of the event. Surprise turns to pleasure or happiness, if the event is or foretells something you like. Disgust greets the noxious or distasteful event. If the event is provocative of aggression, surprise yields to anger. And if the event poses a threat which you cannot obviously mitigate, you feel fear. Fear is the most common sequel to surprise, perhaps because unexpected events are often dangerous, and many people come to associate anything unexpected with danger. In a later chapter we will show how the recognition of fear and surprise can be confused because of similarities in their facial manifestations.

Because the experience of surprise is brief, with another emotion quickly following it, the face often shows a *blend* of surprise and the subsequent emotion. Similarly, if one is already experiencing an emotion when a surprising event occurs, a blend is evident on the face. A keen observer who pays attention to fleeting facial expressions· might catch a pure surprise expression. Most of us, however, are more familiar with the appearance of surprise in combination with elements of a second emotion. Thus, the wide-open eyes of surprise may endure for an instant, as a grin spreads over the lower face. Or the raised brow of surprise may momentarily appear with the stretched-back mouth of fear. In the next chapter we will show fear-surprise blends; in subsequent chapters we will show surprise-disgust, surprise-anger, and surprise-happy blends.

Surprise varies in intensity from mild to extreme, depending upon the event itself. The unexpected appearance of a wife in her husband's office would presumably be less surprising than the unexpected appearance of an old childhood friend not seen for years. The *startle* reaction has been considered to be the most extreme form of surprise, but it has special characteristics which distinguish it from surprise. The startle reaction differs from surprise in facial appearance. The eyes blink, the head moves back, the lips retract, and there is a "jumping" or "starting" movement. A sudden and extreme change in stimulation, best exemplified by the sound of a gun or a car backfiring, produces the startle reaction. Unlike surprise, where correct anticipation of an event prevents the experience, the startle reaction can be elicited by events you anticipate. Successive loud reports from a gun continue to call forth the startle reaction, although the feeling and appearance diminish. Unlike the surprise experience, which is neither pleasant nor unpleasant, the startle experience is usually unpleasant. No one likes the way it feels. Although people speak of a startling idea, or being startled by what someone said, this may be a figure of speech. It is not clear whether a person can be startled by anything other than a sudden extreme sound, sight, or touch. You may be extremely surprised by what someone says, show an extreme surprise facial expression, and describe the occurrence as startling. Thus, the term *startle* is used to describe the most extreme surprise reaction, and also for a reaction related to but different from surprise. The startle reaction is also closely related to fear, and in the next chapter when we distinguish fear from surprise, we will also further explain the relationship of the startle to both surprise and fear.

The experience of each of the emotions we will discuss can be enjoyable. It is obvious that happiness is an enjoyable emotion, but surprise, fear, anger, disgust, and even sadness also can be enjoyed though obviously they usually are not. Some people rarely enjoy being happy, but instead feel guilty or ashamed of their pleasure. Enjoyment of the emotions, or the inability ever to enjoy them, is probably the result of learning during childhood, but little is known about just how this occurs.

Certainly, there are people who love being surprised. A surprise party, a surprise gift, a surprise visit delights them. They organize their lives, in part at least, so that there is a high likelihood of being surprised. They seek the novel. Taken to the extreme, a person "addicted" to surprise, who thrives on it more than any other emotion, would have to sacrifice planning. His life might well tend to be disorganized so that he did not through anticipation eliminate the chance of surprise.

There are also people who can't stand being surprised. They will tell you, "Please don't ever surprise me," even if the surprise is going to be a pleasant one. They don't wish to be subject to the unexpected. They organize their lives to reduce novelty and to avoid experiences in which they will not know what is coming next. Taken to an extreme, if a person can't tolerate surprise, he will be overly planned, calculating every contingency, never recognizing the unexpected if he can construe it as predictable. Imagine the dilemma of a scientist who dreads surprises; he can only prove or disprove his hypotheses but can never discover anything he didn't anticipate.

The Appearance of Surprise

Photographs of two people, Patricia and John, are used in this and the next five chapters to show the facial blueprints. Appendix I describes what we considered in making these photographs, how the pictures were made, and who these two people are.

There is a distinctive appearance in each of the three facial areas during surprise. The eyebrows are raised, the eyes are opened wide, and the jaw drops open, parting the lips.

the surprise brow

The eyebrows appear curved and high. In Figure 4, you see Patricia's surprise brow (B) and her normal or neutral brow (A). The skin below the

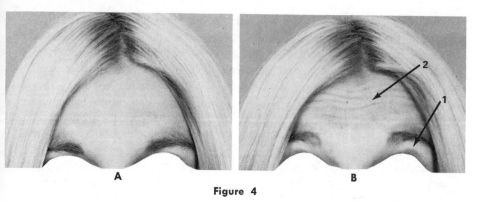

Figure 4

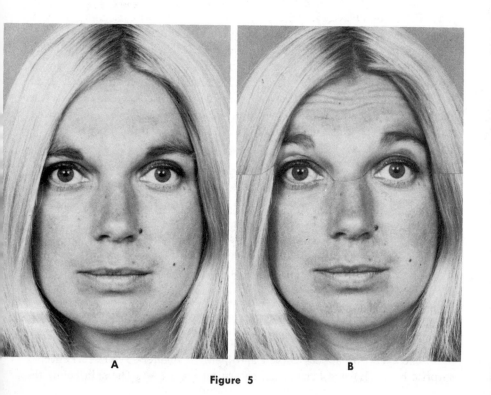

Figure 5

brow has been stretched by the lifting of the brow, and is more visible than usual (Arrow 1). The lifting of the eyebrows produces long horizontal wrinkles across the forehead (Arrow 2). Not everyone shows these wrinkles. Most young children do not show them, even when the eyebrows are raised, and some adults do not either. Some people have horizontal wrinkles—lines etched permanently in their faces—even when the eyebrows have not been moved, but this is unusual until middle age. If there are such permanent wrinkles in the neutral face, the wrinkles become still deeper and more apparent when the eyebrows are raised in surprise.

Although the surprise brow is usually joined by wide-open eyes and dropped jaw, it sometimes appears in an otherwise neutral face. When this happens, the facial expression no longer signifies an emotion; it has different meanings, some of which are related to surprise. In Figure 5, you see the surprise brow with the rest of the face uninvolved or neutral (B), and a full neutral face (A). When the brow is held in place for a few seconds or more, this is an *emblem* which means doubt or questioning. Frequently it is shown by a person who is listening to what someone is saying; it registers without words a question or doubt about what is being said. The questioning or doubting may be serious or not; often this emblem will express mock doubt, the listener's incredulity or amazement about what she has just heard. If joined by a head movement, sideways or backwards, it is an exclamation. If the surprise brow is joined by a disgust mouth, then the meaning of the emblem changes slightly to skeptical disbelief, or if the head rotates back and forth, incredulous exclamation (see Figure 28, Chapter 6).

Figure 5 reveals something else that is very important when looking at facial expressions. Patricia seems to show the doubt or questioning across her entire face; but this is a composite photograph. The brow is the only part of the face that has been changed from the neutral picture on the left. If you cover the brow with your hand, you can see that this is so. With many facial expressions a change in just one area gives the impression that the rest of the facial features have changed as well.

If the surprise brow is held very briefly, still other meanings are conveyed. If it occurs with a tilt of the head or a slight movement of the head up and down, it is a greeting emblem, what has been called an eyebrow-flash, seen throughout Melanesia, and claimed by one investigator to be universal. The quick brow-raise may also be employed as a conversational punctuator. While a person is talking she may quickly raise and lower her brows to emphasize a particular word or phrase. The expression accents the spoken word as italics do the written word. Other brow movements and movements in other parts of the face are also used as punctuators, and we will mention some of these later.

Figure 6

the eyes

The eyes are opened wide during surprise, with the lower eyelids relaxed and the upper eyelids raised. In Figure 6, Patricia and John show the open eyes of surprise; for each the surprise eyes are shown on the left and the neutral eyes on the right. Note that in surprise the white of the eyes—the sclera —shows above the iris—the colored center part of the eye. The sclera may also show below the iris, but this will depend upon how deeply set the eyes are, and whether the jaw has been dropped so far open as to stretch the skin below the eye. Thus, the white of the eye showing below the iris is not as reliable an indication of surprise as is the white above the iris.

Usually the surprise eye is accompanied by the surprise brow or the surprise mouth or both, but it can occur alone. When the upper eyelid is raised, exposing the sclera without any other involvement of the brows or mouth, it is almost always a very brief action lasting a fraction of a second. This widened eye can be a momentary show of interest, or can occur in addition to or in place of a word like "wow." The widened eye can also be used as a conversational punctuator, accenting a particular word as it is spoken.

lower face

The jaw drops during surprise, causing the lips and teeth to part. Figure 7 shows that the opened mouth of surprise is relaxed, not tense; the lips are not tightened, nor are they stretched back. Instead, the mouth looks as if it actually fell open. The mouth may be just slightly open, moderately open as shown in Figure 7, or more widely open, and this varies with just how intense the surprise is. We will show an example of this variation below.

The jaw may be dropped without any movement in the rest of the face. Figure 8 shows the surprise lower face, the dropped jaw, with the rest of the face uninvolved, and for comparison the neutral face. The meaning of this action is to be dumbfounded. It could occur if Patricia were actually dumbfounded, or as an emblem when she wants to state that she felt dumbfounded

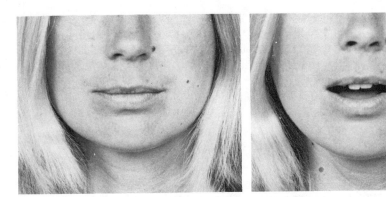

Figure 7

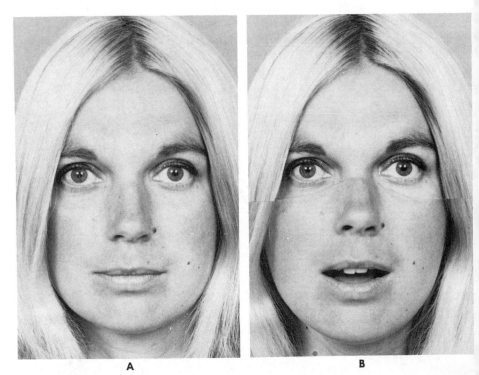

A   B

Figure 8

at some other time, or as a mock expression when she wants to play at being dumbfounded. Figure 8, like Figure 5, demonstrates how changing one part of the face creates the impression of a total change. Look at the eye area in 8B; it probably looks a little more surprised than the eyes in the neutral picture 8A. But this is another composite photograph; if you cover the mouths of both pictures with your hands, you will see that the eyes and brow/forehead are the same in both pictures. (In discussing Figures 5 and 8 we used the terms *emblem, mock expression,* and *punctuator.* If you don't remember how we defined these terms, please check back in Chapter 2).

slight to extreme surprise

The experience of surprise varies in intensity, and the face reflects the differences. Although there are slight changes in the brows (going up a bit higher) and the eyes (widening and opening a bit more), the major clue to the intensity of the surprise is in the lower face. Slight surprise is shown in

Figure 9

A	B

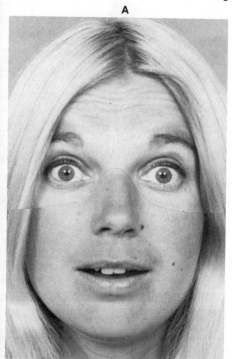 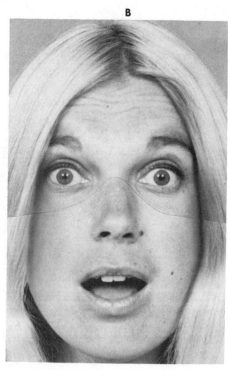

Figure 9A, moderate surprise in 9B. The brows and eyes are identical in the two pictures; only the extent of the jaw-drop has been varied. In more extreme surprise the mouth would be opened even wider. With extreme surprise there often will be an exclamation such as "oh" or "wow."

four types of surprise

Surprise may be shown in just two areas of the face, with the third area uninvolved. Each of these two-area surprise faces has a slightly different meaning. Figure 10 shows these four types of surprise. Before we explain what message we think each picture conveys and how the differences in facial appearance are responsible for these different messages, you might look at each picture and ask yourself, "What is the message?" and "How does this face differ in appearance from the other faces?"

In 10A, Patricia is showing a questioning surprise, a rather uncertain surprise. The words that go with it might be something like "Is that so?" or "Oh, really?" This facial expression is exactly the same face as 10D, except that the surprise mouth has been covered with a neutral mouth. If you cover the mouths in 10A and 10D with your fingers, you will see that they are the same picture except for the mouths. Surprise looks questioning when only the eyes and brow movements of the full-face surprise expression occur.

In 10B, Patricia shows astonished surprise, or amazed surprise. The words that go with this expression might be something like "What?" or a vocalization such as "Aauuh" with a sudden inspiration of breath. If you cover the brow and forehead in 10B and in 10D with your fingers, you will see that they are the same picture except for the brow/forehead. Surprise looks amazed when only the eyes and mouth movements of the full-face surprise expression occur.

In 10C, Patricia shows a more dazed surprise, or less interested surprise, or surprise as shown by someone who is exhausted or drugged. If you cover the eyes in 10C and 10D, you will see that they are the same picture except for the eyes. Surprise looks dazed when only the brow and mouth movements from the full-face surprise expression occur.

Figure 10D shows the full surprise expression, with all three facial areas involved. Its message is—surprise.

Review

Figure 11 shows the full-face surprise expressions. Note each of the distinctive clues to surprise.

Figure 10

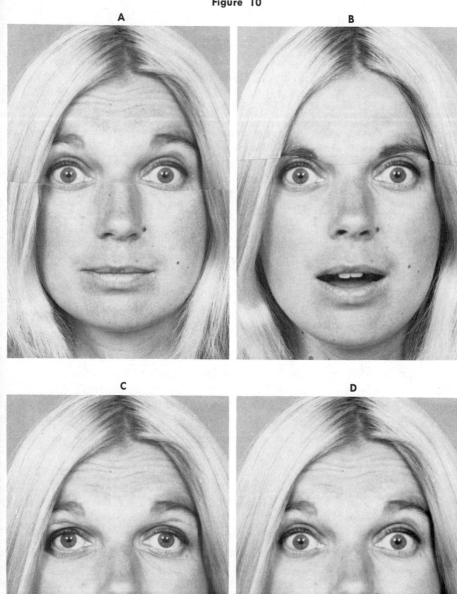

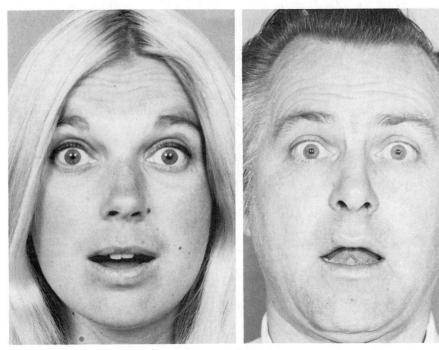

Figure 11

—The brows are raised, so that they are curved and high.

—The skin below the brow is stretched.

—Horizontal wrinkles go across the forehead.

—The eyelids are opened; the upper lid is raised and the lower lid drawn down; the white of the eye—the sclera—shows above the iris, and often below as well.

—The jaw drops open so that the lips and teeth are parted, but there is no tension or stretching of the mouth.

making faces

Another way to review what you have learned about the surprise facial expressions is actually to construct some of the faces you have seen in this chapter. Cut out the four pieces of the neutral facial expressions of John and Patricia on the back cover. Now you have what you need to make some of the different surprise facial expressions.

1. Take the C pieces and place them over the faces in Figure 11. What is the expression? You have seen Patricia's face before, but not John's expression. It is questioning or disbelief (Figure 5).

2. Put B over the faces in Figure 11. What is the expression? You saw Patricia's expression before in Figure 8, and John's is the same. It is dumbfounded.

3. Put A on the pictures and then put D on as well. This is a facial expression you haven't seen before but which was discussed on page 40. You have just the surprise eyes, and if the expression occurs for a moment, it means interest or an exclamation. Leave D where it is and interchange A and B. This will give you the impression of the eyes shifting back and forth from neutral to surprise, as they would in life.

4. Leave just A on. The expression is astonishment (Figure 10B). Now put D back on and remove A. The expression is questioning surprise. By switching back and forth between A and D you can see most dramatically how the meanings of the expressions change.

5

fear

People fear harm. The harm may be physical or psychological, or both. The physical harm may vary from something minor, such as a vaccination puncture, to actual life-endangering injuries. Psychological harm can also vary from minor insults or disappointments to extreme assaults on one's well-being, rejection of one's love, attacks on one's worth. The psychological harm may involve damage (to self-esteem, confidence, sense of security), or loss of love, friendship, possessions, etc. Harm may involve both physical pain and psychological suffering; for example, a teenager being beaten up by a rival in view of his girlfriend may be both physically and psychologically bruised.

Survival depends on learning to avoid or escape from situations that cause severe pain and the likelihood of physical injury. You learn to anticipate danger early. You evaluate what is occurring, alert to the possibility of harm. Very often you feel fear in advance of harm. You fear both real and imagined threats of harm. You fear any event, person, animal, thing, or idea that appears dangerous. If you are told that next week you are going to have to undergo a series of extremely painful rabies injections, you are likely to feel fear well before the pain from the first needle. If you see the boss storm in to work, obviously angry at something and ready to explode, you may well become afraid before his attention turns to you. The fear of danger, the anticipation of even physical pain, can often be more miserable than the pain itself. Often, of course, the fear of danger mobilizes efforts to avoid or diminish the impending harm.

Fear is so often experienced in advance of harm—you are so successful in spotting danger before pain hits—that it is possible to forget that you can be caught unawares. Thinking, planning, evaluating, and anticipating do not always protect or even warn you. Sometimes you are harmed without notice, and when that happens you feel fear without much, if any, prior thought about what is happening. Fear may then be experienced virtually simultaneously with harm. A sudden sharp pain causes fear. You do not pause to think about whether you are hurting or what is hurting. You hurt and are afraid. If the pain continues and there is time to evaluate what is occurring, you may become even more afraid—"Am I having a heart attack?" If you burn your hand in the flame of the kitchen stove, you feel pain and fear (and perhaps distress as well—see Chapter 9). Just as you would recoil without pausing to consider why it is that the stove was on when you thought it was off, so you would feel fear without pausing to evaluate how badly you were burned, cut, etc. Fear experienced simultaneously with harm can also occur with psychological suffering. If the boss comes up to the office worker who is dozing off at his desk and shouts, "You're fired, you lazy idiot," fear is experienced (and perhaps the startle reaction as well). The person does not need time to consider what is happening, although such consideration may cause the fear to increase—"Oh my God, I'm not going to be able to pay my rent." Or another emotion may take the place of fear or blend with it— "He's got no right to talk to me like that—after I spent all of last night working to meet his deadline."

Fear differs from surprise in three important ways. Fear is a terrible experience, and surprise is not. Surprise is not necessarily pleasant or unpleasant, but even mild fear is unpleasant. Strong fear—terror—is probably the most traumatic or toxic of all emotions. It is accompanied by many changes in the body. The skin of a terrified person may become pale. He may sweat. His breathing may become rapid, his heart pound, his pulse throb, his stomach may become queasy or tense. His bladder or bowel may open, and his hands tremble. He may find it hard not to move backwards away from the threatening event, and even if he is frozen in immobility his posture is one of withdrawal. You cannot be extremely afraid for long periods of time, for this state of terror depletes and exhausts you.

The second way fear differs from surprise is that you can be afraid of something familiar that you know full well is going to happen. You can know that the dentist is about to call you into his office—there is no surprise in store for you, because he has hurt you before—but you can be very much afraid. You can be waiting to be called to the podium to deliver a lecture, or standing in the wings waiting for your cue to appear on stage in a play, and have stage fright even if you are an experienced lecturer or actor. There are many such experiences, causing some people to experience fear the second, tenth, or twentieth time they know they are going to be in a particular situation. When fear is felt suddenly, when there is no anticipation of danger but the fear is simultaneous with harm, the experience may be tinged with surprise. Thus, in many of these sudden fear experiences, you will experience a blend of surprise and fear or of startle and fear.

A third way in which fear differs from surprise is in its duration. Surprise is the briefest emotion, but unfortunately fear is not. Surprise always has a short duration. Unanticipated fear, or fear experienced simultaneously with harm, can have a short duration, but fear can also occur gradually. Home late at night alone in the house, the first slight sound can start slight apprehension. As you think about what may be occurring, as you magnify and elaborate each subsequent squeak of the floorboards, your apprehension may slowly grow to fear, or even terror. When you are surprised you feel surprised for only a brief time, only until you have evaluated what the surprising event was. Fear can last much longer; you can fully know the nature of the fear-inspiring event and remain quite afraid. The whole time the airplane is in flight you may be sitting in fear, anticipating a crash. There is a limit to human endurance, however, and fear will exhaust you physically if it is experienced in its most extreme state continuously. Surprise usually recedes quickly as you evaluate the event and move into one or another emotion, depending upon how you feel about what surprised you. Fear lingers. Even after the danger has passed, you may still feel the sensations of fear. If the danger is extremely quick in coming and going, so that you don't know what a spot you were in until you are no longer in it, as in a near miss in an automobile, you may experience the fear only afterward.

Fear varies in intensity from apprehension to terror. How intense the experience of fear is depends upon the event or your appraisal of the event. When the fear is experienced simultaneously with harm, then the extent of the fear will likely be a reflection of how severe the pain is. When the pain continues, the fear may become more intense if you anticipate even worse pain or intractable pain. When the fear experienced is in response to danger, to the threat of harm rather than to harm itself, the intensity of the fear depends upon your evaluation of the extent of the impending harm and your chances of coping with it, avoiding it, reducing it, surviving it. In a threatening situation you may merely feel apprehensive if you know you can avoid the threat by flight, or if you know that the pain will not be truly harmful. But when flight is not possible, and if the harm anticipated is great, your apprehension may turn to terror as you become immobilized, frozen in a posture of helplessness.

Fear may be followed by any of the other emotions, or by no emotion at all. You may become angry, attacking the agent that posed the danger, or angry or disgusted with yourself for having placed yourself in jeopardy, or for having responded to jeopardy with fear. Sadness may follow fear if the harm is enduring, or if in other ways the danger had a regrettable consequence. There may be an extended sequence of emotions; you may feel fear, then anger, then sadness, etc. Fear may also be experienced as a blend with another emotion if the event provokes two feelings at once. For example, someone threatens you and you feel both afraid of the attack and angry at the provocation.

Happiness may also follow fear. You can be happy that the threat has been avoided or, even if the harm has been endured, you can feel happy that it is over. Some people are able to enjoy the emotion of fear. The threat of harm is a challenge that is thrilling and has purpose. Such people are called brave, courageous, or daring. They may be soldiers, mountain climbers, gamblers, race-track drivers, etc. Many more people enjoy pseudo-fear experiences, such as those offered in an amusement park roller-coaster. There is a threat of harm, but it is known not to be a real threat, and there is little the person can do to meet the threat. There are, of course, people for whom fear is extremely difficult to experience. They cannot even tolerate a pseudo-fear experience. Fear is so overwhelming for them that they plan their lives with great caution, seeking various protections or avoiding that which they know will frighten them. Such people gain little satisfaction from enduring and surviving fear; the fear experience is altogether too toxic an experience for them.

The Appearance of Fear

There is a distinctive appearance in each of the three facial areas during fear. The eyebrows are raised and drawn together; the eyes are open and the lower lid is tensed; and the lips are stretched back.

the fear brow

The eyebrows appear raised and straightened. Figure 12 shows the fear brow (B) and the surprise brow (A). Note that in the fear brow, the brows are lifted (1) as they are in the surprise brow, but in addition to the lift they are drawn together so that the inner corners of the brow (2) are closer together in fear than in surprise. The drawing together of the brow gives a more straightened appearance to the outer corners of the eyebrow in fear than in surprise. In the fear brow there are usually horizontal wrinkles across the forehead (3), but typically they do not run across the entire forehead, as they do in surprise (4).

Although the fear brow is commonly joined by the fear eyes and fear mouth, it sometimes appears in an otherwise neutral face. When this happens the facial expression conveys a message related to fear. In Figure 13B John's expression is composed of the fear brow with the rest of the face uninvolved

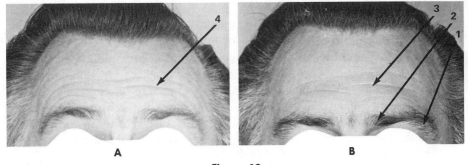

Figure 12

Figure 13

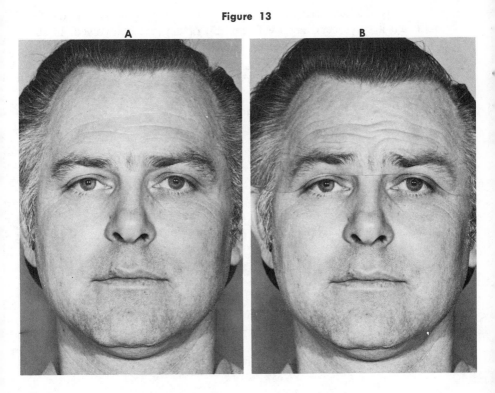

or neutral. Figure 13A shows, for comparison, John's completely neutral expression. When the brow is held in the fear position, as in 13B, the meaning of the expression is worry or slight apprehension, or controlled fear. Figure 13 again demonstrates that changing only one area of the face changes the total impression. It appears that the worry is shown also in John's eyes and even a bit in his mouth. But this is a composite photograph in which the fear brow has been pasted over the forehead of the neutral picture on the left. If you cover with your hand the brow/forehead in the two pictures in this figure, you will see that the eyes and mouth are the same.

the fear eye

The eyes are opened and tense during fear, the upper eyelid raised and the lower eyelid tense. Figure 14 shows the fear eyes (A), neutral eyes (B), and surprise eyes (C). Note that in both the fear and surprise eyes the upper lid is raised, exposing the sclera (white) above the iris (1). Although fear and surprise share this upper lid characteristic, they differ in regard to the lower lid, which is tense and raised in fear (2) and relaxed in surprise. The tension and raising of the lower eyelid in fear may be sufficient to cover part of the iris (3).

Usually the fear eye will be shown with the fear brow and the fear mouth, but it may occur alone with the rest of the face uninvolved. In such an instance it will be a brief expression, in which the eyes momentarily take

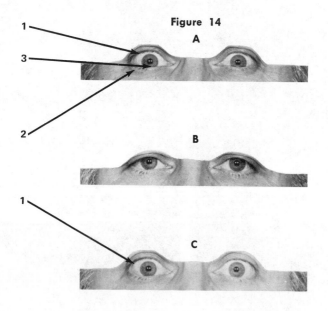

Figure 14

on the fear appearance. If this happens it is usually a genuine expression of fear, but the fear is either slight or being controlled.

the fear mouth

The mouth opens in fear, but the lips are tense and may be drawn back tightly. In Figure 15, Patricia shows two types of fear mouth (A and B), and for comparison the surprise mouth (C) and neutral mouth (D). The fear mouth shown in 15A is quite similar to the surprise mouth (15C), but it differs in an important way—the lips are not relaxed as they are in surprise; there is tension in the upper lip and the beginning trace of the corners of the lips being drawn back. In the other type of fear mouth (15B), the lips are stretched and tense with the corners drawn back.

Figure 15

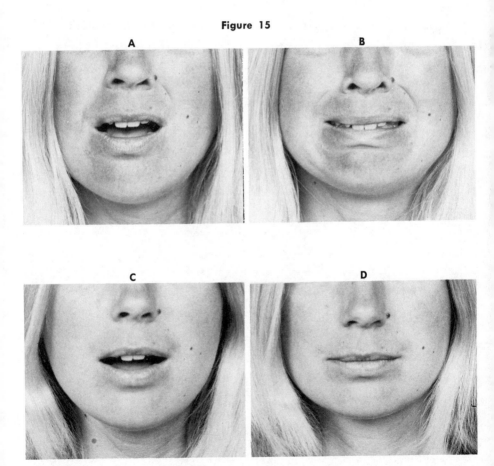

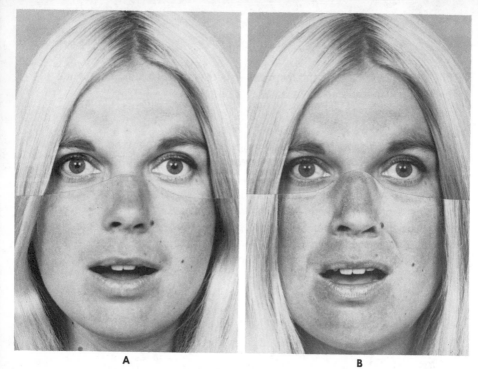

A   B

Figure 16

Figure 17

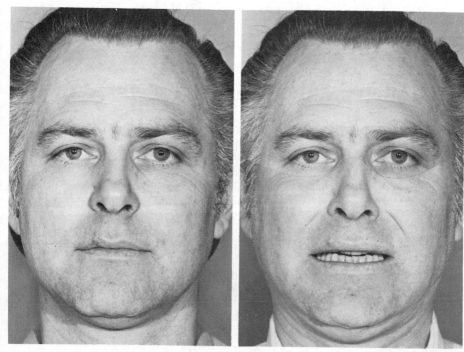

Although the fear mouth is usually joined by the fear eyes and brow, they can each occur alone, and their meaning then differs. In Figure 16 Patricia shows the more open fear mouth, with the rest of the face neutral on the right, and for comparison the surprise mouth, with the rest of the face neutral on the left. When the face on the right is shown, it means worry or apprehension; it refers to a momentary feeling at the beginning of a fear experience. In contrast, the facial expression on the left, discussed in the previous chapter, shows a dumbfounded expression and may occur when the person actually is dumbfounded or is playing at being dumbfounded. The more stretched fear mouth may also occur with the rest of the face uninvolved, but when this happens it will usually be a momentary, quick expression, in which the lips are stretched back and then return. Figure 17 shows this stretched fear mouth with the rest of the face uninvolved, and for comparison John's neutral face. If this expression flashes on and off the face quickly, it could mean that John is actually afraid but trying not to show it; or that John is anticipating a fearful or painful experience; or that John is not feeling fear but referring to or mentioning a fearful or painful event. An example of this last, emblematic fear expression is a person, in describing a recent automobile accident, quickly flashing the stretch mouth, referring to the fear or pain he experienced then.

slight to extreme fear

Fear varies in its intensity from apprehension to terror, and the face reflects these differences. Intensity is shown in the eyes, with the raising of the upper lid and the tensing of the lower lid increasing as the intensity of the fear increases. Even more evident are the changes in the fear mouth. In Figure 18 Patricia shows increasing intensity of fear, clockwise, starting with 18A, by increased stretching and opening of the mouth. Though 18C may seem more fearful than 18A, once again these are composite photographs and the fear eyes and forehead are exactly the same; only the mouth differs.

two-way fear expressions

Fear may be shown in just two areas of the face, with the third area uninvolved. Each of these two-way fear faces has a slightly different meaning. Figure 19 shows the two types of two-way fear expressions. John's expression in 19A is apprehensive fear, as if John is just realizing that a harmful event is impending. This expression has this meaning because the lower face is not involved—fear is shown only in the brow and eyes. Compare John's expression in 19A with the picture of John in Figure 13B. John is apprehensive in both, but more apprehensive in Figure 19A than in Figure 13B,

Figure 18

A

B

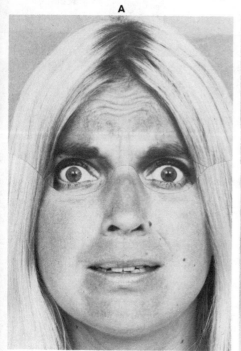

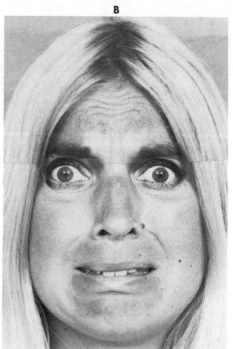

C

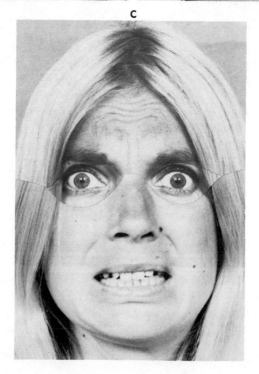

Figure 19

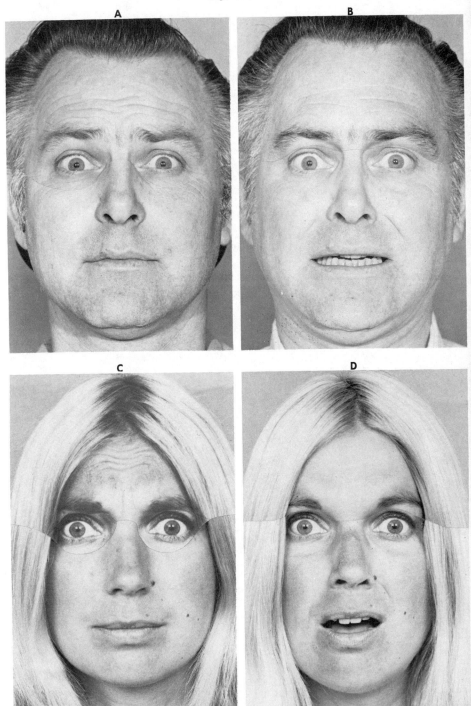

A

B

C

D

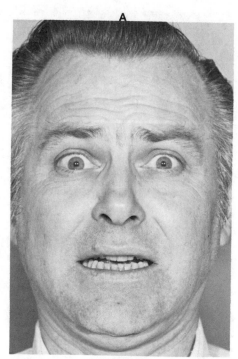

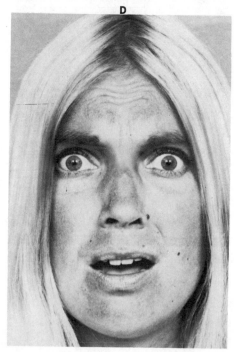

Figure 20

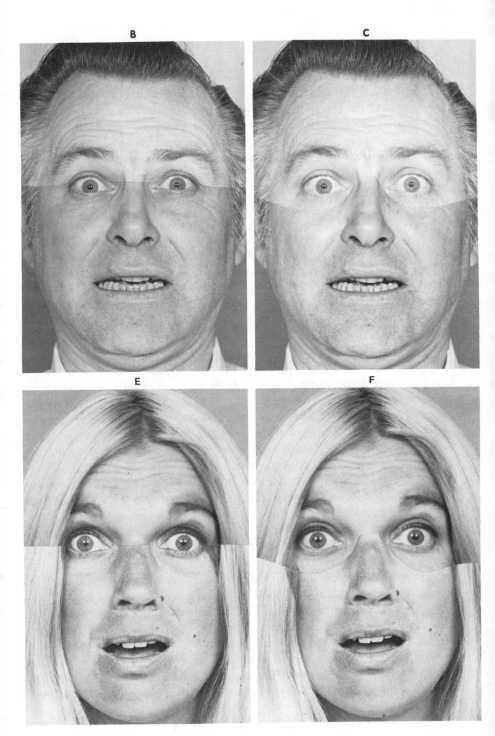

59

because fear is only in the brow in Figure 13B, but in the eyes and brow in Figure 19A.

John's expression in 19B shows more of a frozen, horrified fear. Interestingly, the intensity of this expression of fear is not reduced by the lack of involvement of the brow (it is a neutral brow). Instead, the absence of brow involvement causes the expression to appear immobilized or frozen.

Patricia shows these different types of fear expressions with some subtle variations. In 19C her expression is apprehensive fear because fear is shown only in the brows and eyes, not in the mouth. It is just the same as John's expression above it (19A). In 19D Patricia's expression is horror. It is like John's expression in 19B because fear is shown in the eyes and mouth only. Her expression differs from John's because Patricia is using the less stretched fear mouth. Her face looks shocked more than horrified because this fear mouth has more similarity to the surprise mouth. Compare this expression of Patricia (19D) with her expression in 16B. She looks only apprehensive, not shocked, in Figure 16B because fear is only in the mouth. The shock element apparent in her expression in 19D comes from the addition of the fear eyes.

blend of fear and surprise

Fear may occur simultaneously with sadness, anger, or disgust; and a blend expression consisting of fear and one of these other emotions can be shown on the face. Fear may also occur partially masked by a happy look, and a blend expression will be shown. These blends of fear with sadness, anger, disgust, or happiness will be presented in subsequent chapters, when each of these other emotions is explained. The most common blend with fear is surprise, because often fearful events are unexpected ones, and it is common to be both surprised and afraid at the same moment, or almost the same moment. In most of these blended expressions, where part of the face shows surprise and part shows fear, the dominant impression is that of fear.

Figure 20 shows two types of fear-surprise blends, and for comparison full-face fear expressions on the left side of the figure. Moving your eyes from left to right, you can see increasing surprise blended with the fear. For both John and Patricia the difference between the pictures on the far left and far right is more apparent than the difference between the adjacent pictures. This is because the pictures that are adjacent differ in only one facial area, while the pictures on the two sides differ from each other in two facial areas.

In 20B the surprise element is only in the forehead and brow, with the rest of the face showing fear. The impression differs very subtly from the picture on the left. In 20E, surprise again is registered only in the brow/forehead, with fear in the rest of the face, but the difference is more apparent from the full-face fear shown to its left. The difference is more apparent for Patricia than John, probably because Patricia shows the more surprise-like mouth. It is also easier to see surprise elements in her blend pictures because of physiognomic differences between her eyes/forehead and John's.

The pictures on the far right of Figure 20 show surprise in both the brow/forehead and eyes, with fear only in the mouth. Though this is the same for both Patricia and John, John's expression (20C) conveys more of a fear message than does Patricia's (20F). Again, this is because of the type of fear mouth in the pictures. John's is the fear mouth that differs most from the surprise mouth. Patricia's fear mouth is the one that is most similar to the surprise mouth. In case you think that Patricia looks totally surprised in 20F, with no fear element blended, compare this picture with her picture in Figure 11, and you will see the difference.

Figure 21 shows two other types of fear-surprise blends. Patricia's expression shows surprise only in the mouth, with fear in the eyes and brow. She looks afraid, but not as afraid as in the straight fear expression shown in 20D.

Figure 21

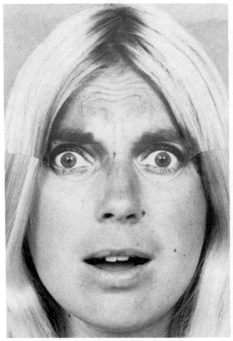 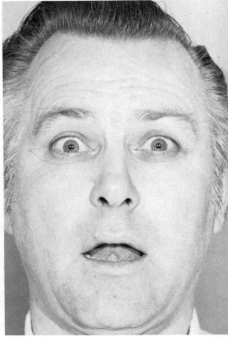

In Figure 21 there is more of a dumbfounded element to Patricia's fear because of the surprise mouth. Compare Patricia's expression in Figure 21 with her expression in 19C. The brows and eyes are the same, but replacing the neutral mouth (Figure 19C) with a surprise mouth (Figure 21) adds an element of fear and changes the apprehensive fear of Figure 19C to a greater but more incredulous fear.

John's expression in Figure 21 shows the last way in which fear and surprise can be blended. In this instance John shows fear only in the eyes. Just the tightening of the lower eyelid changes his expression from surprise to fearful surprise. Compare John's expression in Figure 21 with his expression in Figure 11, in order to see the difference between this fear-surprise blend and the straight surprise expression.

Review

Figure 22 shows two full-face fear expressions. Note each of the distinctive clues to fear.

Figure 22

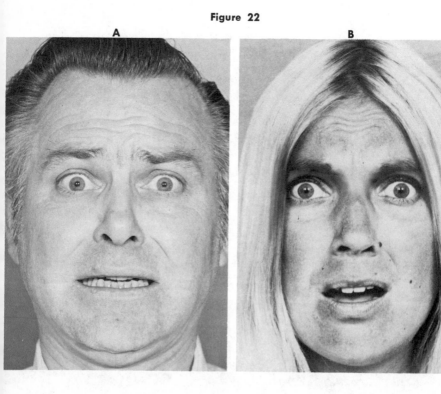

—The brows are raised and drawn together.

—The wrinkles in the forehead are in the center, not across the entire forehead.

—The upper eyelid is raised, exposing sclera, and the lower eyelid is tensed and drawn up.

—The mouth is open and the lips are either tensed slightly and drawn back or stretched and drawn back.

making faces

1. Put the C pieces over the faces in Figure 22. What is the expression? You have seen John's expression before in Figure 13, and Patricia's is the same, if a little more subtle. Worry, slight apprehension, controlled fear are the possible messages.

2. Put B over the faces in Figure 22. The expression? Patricia's expression means worry or apprehension (Figure 16B). John's expression may have this meaning, or it may be controlled fear, or if it flashes on and off very quickly, it may be an emblematic fear expression (Figure 17).

3. Put both A and D on the faces in Figure 22. This is a facial expression you weren't shown before but which was discussed on page 52. It has the fear eyes, which might be shown momentarily in a highly controlled fear, or a very slight fear.

4. Take off A. The expression is the same as in the left side of Figure 19—apprehensive fear.

5. Remove D and replace A. This is the expression shown on the right side of Figure 19; it is the more horrified, frozen fear. By interchanging A and D you can best see how the meaning of the expression changes.

flashing faces

Another way to practice what you have learned is to flash some of the photographs before your eyes and try to identify the correct emotion. You can do this, using selected figures from the preceding chapters. The procedure is somewhat complex—but most people find it a useful step to actually become able to spot these facial expressions in real life.

You will need:

1. A partner; your partner will select photos and flash them for you.

2. An L-shaped cardboard mask; your partner will need to cover up other photos that may be on the same page so you will see only the face being flashed.

3. A list of the faces to be flashed and a presentation order; the basic list is given below but your partner will need to re-order this list so you won't know which photo is coming next—and, of course, it's important to know the order of presentation so you can compare your answers later.

4. An answer sheet, numbered from 1 to 22, for you to record your answers.

Your task is to figure out which emotion is shown in each picture.

List of Faces for Flashing Faces, Practice One:

Figure Number:	*Answers:*
5A	Neutral
9A	Slight Surprise
10A	Questioning Surprise
10B	Astonished Surprise
10C	Dazed Surprise
10D	Full Face Surprise
11, right photo	Full Face Surprise
13A	Neutral
13B	Worry
16B	Worry or Apprehension
17, right photo	Fear Emblem or Controlled Fear
18B	Fear
19A	Apprehensive Fear
19B	Horrified Fear
19C	Apprehensive Fear
19D	Horrified or Shocked Fear
20C	Fear-Surprise Blend
20F	Fear-Surprise Blend
21, left photo	Fear-Surprise Blend
21, right photo	Fear-Surprise Blend
22A	Full Face Fear
22B	Full Face Fear

Your partner should show each picture for only *one* second. He/she should then quickly remove it from view and find and mask the next photo to be presented while you record your answer. Guess if you have to, but go through all 22 presentations before checking your answers.

If you get them all right the first time, you're doing very well. You're an expert on FEAR and SURPRISE! If you missed some expressions, re-read what the text said about those particular figures. Then have your partner re-order the photos and try the complete set again.

If you don't get them all right the first time, don't be discouraged. Many perceptive people take three or four attempts to get them all correct.

After Chapter 7 and Chapter 9, you'll find additional exercises with flashing faces—including additional emotions. You'll find succeeding exercises much easier if you've thoroughly mastered FEAR and SURPRISE at this point, before going on.

6

disgust

Disgust is a feeling of aversion. The taste of something you want to spit out, even the thought of eating something distasteful, can make you disgusted. A smell that you want to block out of your nasal passage, or move away from, calls forth disgust. And again, even the thought of how something repulsive might smell can bring out strong disgust. The sight of something you think might be offensive to taste or smell can make you disgusted. Sounds might also make you disgusted, if they are related to an abhorrent event. And touch, the feel of something offensive, such as a slimy object, can make you disgusted.

The tastes, smells, touches that you find disgusting are by no means universally so. What is repulsive to people in one culture may be attractive to people in another culture. This is most easily exemplified with foods—dog meat, bull's testicles, raw fish, calves' brains are by no means universally appetizing. Even within a culture there is no unanimity about what is disgusting. Within our own society some delight in raw oysters, others can't even bear to see them eaten. Within a family there may be disagreement; children often find certain foods disgusting which they will later come to find appetizing.

Disgust usually involves getting-rid-of and getting-away-from responses. Removing the object or oneself from the object is the goal. Nausea and vomiting can occur with the most extreme, uncontrolled, primitive experience of disgust. This reaction can be brought on not only by tasting something repulsive, but by the sight or smell of something repulsive. Of course, nausea and vomiting occur without disgust, and likewise disgust occurs without nausea or vomiting.

It is not only tastes, smells, and touches or the thought, sight, or sound of them that can bring forth disgust but also the actions and appearance of people, or even ideas. People can be offensive in their appearance; to look at them may be distasteful. Some people experience disgust when seeing a deformed, crippled person, or an ugly person. An injured person with an exposed wound may be disgusting. The sight of blood or the witnessing of surgery makes some people disgusted. Certain human actions are also disgusting; you may be revolted by what a person does. A person who mistreats or tortures a dog or cat may be the object of disgust. A person who indulges in what others consider sexual perversion may be disgusting. A philosophy of life or way of treating people that is considered debasing can make those who regard it that way feel disgusted.

Disgust can vary in intensity. At the opposite end from the nausea-vomiting disgust is a mild dislike, a turning-away from the object of disgust. In this mild disgust, the getting-away-from or getting-rid-of impulses may be contained or not acted upon, but there is dislike for the object. You might have a mild reaction of disgust to the smell of a new dish prepared by your host, but be able to bring yourself to try it. A person with rancid body odor might make you feel slight disgust; you would dislike contact with him, but be able to manage it. When you hear how your friend disciplined his child, you might feel mild disgust if you disapproved of his method, but your friendship might be able to survive it; you might still be able to have contact with him.

Contempt is a close relative of disgust, but it differs in some ways. Contempt is only experienced about people or the actions of people, but not about tastes, smells, or touches. Stepping onto dog droppings might call forth disgust, but never contempt; the idea of eating calves' brains might be disgusting, but it would not evoke contempt. You might, however, feel contemptuous toward people who eat such disgusting things, for in contempt there is an element of condescension toward the object of contempt. Disdainful in disliking the persons or their actions, you feel superior (usually morally) to them. Their offense is degrading, but you need not necessarily get away from them, as you would in disgust. Scorn is a variant of contempt, in which the object of contempt is derided for his failings, often with some element of humor which amuses the person showing the scorn and hurts the recipient.

Often disgust or contempt will be experienced together with anger. You can be angry at someone for being disgusting. For example, if a man drinks too much at a party and begins acting in a sloppy way, his wife may be both disgusted and angry, angry that he is being disgusting. Or the child molester may be the object of both disgust for his sexual act and anger for his moral wrongdoing. If a person's actions make you disgusted rather than angry, it is usually because they pose no threat; your response is to get away from him rather than to defend yourself or attack him. Often disgust will be used to mask anger, because in parts of our society there is a taboo against expressing anger. Paradoxically, people may well prefer to be the recipient of anger than of disgust. If you are disgusting, you are repulsive in your offense. Whether you prefer to cause disgust or anger depends upon the intensity of the disgust or anger, and whether it is seen as aimed at a particular act or at you yourself.

Disgust can blend not only with anger but also with surprise, fear, sadness, and happiness. Each of these reactions will be discussed and shown. People can enjoy disgust, although it is probably not one of the most frequent patterns of affect enjoyment. Some people may even seek a bad smell or taste, flirting with disgust for the pleasure they obtain in being disgusted by something. In many cultures children are discouraged from curiosity about matters which might cause them or others to feel disgust. They are trained to be ashamed of enjoying feeling repulsed. Those adults who find some pleasure in being disgusted may hide this from others, they may feel guilty about what they regard as a perversion, or they may not even realize they enjoy being disgusted. Much more common, and more socially acceptable than enjoying disgust, is the affect pattern of enjoying contempt. People who are full of contempt for others are often the object of respect and admiration because of the power and principle implied in their disdain and distaste. Some people perfect contemptuousness as their predominant interpersonal style: It is displayed toward everyone worthy of their contempt. Haughty, smug, and superior, they look down at the world and may enjoy status for maintaining that lofty posture. Many people, of course, cannot enjoy feeling contemptuous. It is dangerous for them to acknowledge such a presumptuous feeling. Some people cannot tolerate the feeling of disgust. The experience is so toxic that even a slight whiff of disgust may precipitate acute nausea.

The Appearance of Disgust

The most important clues to disgust are manifested in the mouth and nose and to a lesser extent in the lower eyelids and eyebrow. The upper lip is raised, while the lower lip may be raised or lowered; the nose is wrinkled; the lower eyelids are pushed up, and the eyebrow is lowered.

the lower face

In Figure 23, Patricia shows that in disgust the upper lip is raised (1), causing a change in the appearance of the tip of the nose. The raised upper lip may or may not be joined by wrinkling along the sides and bridge of the nose (2). The more extreme the disgust, the more likely it is that the nose-

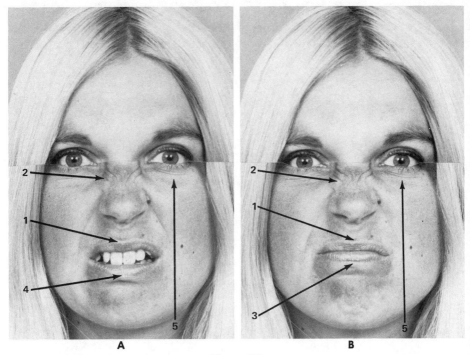

Figure 23

wrinkling will also be apparent. The lower lip may be raised and slightly forward (3), or lowered and slightly forward (4). The cheeks are raised, and this produces a change in the appearance of the lower eyelid, narrowing the opening of the eye and producing many lines and folds below the eye (5). Though the eyebrow is typically down in disgust, this is a fairly unimportant element. Patricia looks disgusted in Figure 23 even though the brow and upper eyelid are from a neutral picture. Compare Figure 23 with Figure 24, in which the brow is down, and you will see that the disgust expression seems more complete, slightly more intense; but the difference between Figures 23 and 24 is not great.

The facial configuration shown in Figure 24 can occur when the person is not actually disgusted, but using an emotion emblem, referring to something disgusting. For example, if Patricia had just said, "When I ate in this restaurant last week, I saw a cockroach," she might be showing one of the disgust emotion emblems. But she would use her face in such a way that it would be obvious to others she is not disgusted now. She might quickly wrinkle her nose, slightly raising her cheeks and upper lip; or she might just raise her upper lip without wrinkling her nose. There are two clues that these are emotion emblems rather than facial expressions of emotion—that Patricia does not actually feel the emotion at this moment, and doesn't want those

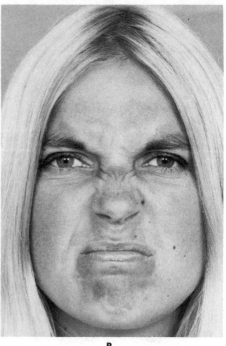

A   B

Figure 24

seeing her to think she does: There is only a partial involvement of the face
—either the nose-wrinkle/cheek-raise/slight lip-raise, or the lip-raise/no
nose-wrinkle, but probably not both. And the expression is a brief flash rather
than one that lasts for a few seconds. A mock-disgust expression might employ the full expression seen in Figure 24, but it would be held on the face
for an unduly long time—playing at being disgusted.

Although not common, some people will use either the nose-wrinkle
or the slight raised upper lip as a conversational punctuator, accenting a particular word or phrase. Earlier we mentioned that some people use the
quickly raised surprise brow or the quickly opened surprise eyelids as conversational punctuators. Later we will see that the lowered, drawn-together
brow of anger is another conversational punctuator, and that the drawn-
together and raised brow of sadness is yet another. In each case the facial
movement functions much like a movement of the hands, to emphasize a
particular word or phrase, italicizing it. Little is known as to why some
people use the face to punctuate rather than or in addition to the hands. And
little is known about whether the particular facial punctuator employed—
surprise brow, disgust nose-wrinkle, or sad brow, etc.—means anything psychologically. It might reflect something about a person's personality; or it
might be the result of his unwittingly imitating a particular person, such as a

parent, in childhood when he acquired speech; or perhaps it is determined by the neuroanatomy.

variations in intensity

Disgust may vary in intensity from slight to extreme. In slight disgust there will be less nose-wrinkling, and the raise of the upper lip will also be less pronounced than in Figure 24. In more extreme disgust, both the nose-wrinkling and the upper-lip raising will be greater than that shown in Figure 24. The nasal-labial fold, the wrinkle running from the nostrils down to the outer lip corners, may become apparent and deeper. In extreme disgust the tongue may come forward and show in the mouth or actually protrude from the mouth (Figure 61).

contempt expressions

Contempt is shown by a variation on the closed-lips disgust mouth. Figure 25 shows three contempt expressions. John shows the unilateral contempt mouth, with slight pressing of the lips and a raising of the corners on one side. Patricia's expression in 25B is essentially the same as John's except that her upper lip is raised on one side, exposing the teeth. This adds the scornful, sneering note to the expression. The picture of Patricia in 25C shows a milder form of contempt, with a barely noticeable lifting of the upper lip on one side of her face. Figure 26 shows a blend of elements of contempt and disgust. The contempt is shown in the tight, slightly raised corners of the mouth with lip pressed against lip. This is very similar to John's face in 25A, except that the expression is bilateral rather than unilateral; the corners are tightened on both sides of Patricia's mouth. The hint of disgust in Patricia's face in Figure 26 comes from the slight forward and upward position of the lower lip, and the slightly wrinkled nose. Compare it with the lower lip in Patricia's picture in 24B and you will see the similarity.

blends

Disgust can blend with surprise. Figure 27 shows a full-face disgust (27A), a surprise face (27B) and a blend of disgust (27C) (lower face and lower eyelid) and surprise (brow/forehead, upper eyelid). This expression might occur if Patricia had been disgusted by something unexpected and the surprise had not completely faded away. More usually, the expression in 27C would not actually be an expression of the blended feelings of disgust and surprise; rather, the surprise brow-raise would have been added as an emblem to emphasize the disgust expression. You might be able to imagine Patricia making a sound like "uucch" in 27A, while in the composite picture in 27C she might be saying, "Oh, my God, how disgusting!"

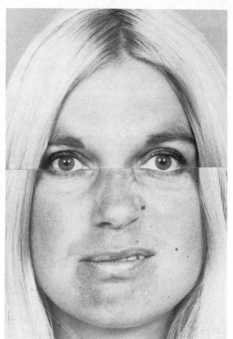

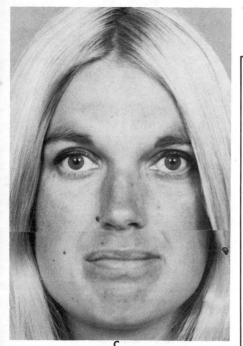

Figure 25

Figure 26

Figure 27

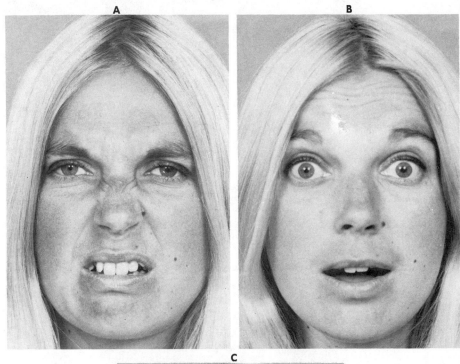

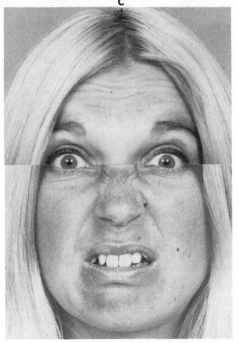

73

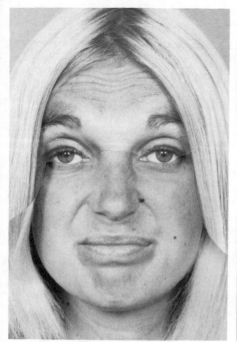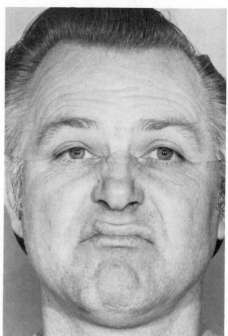

Figure 28

The elements of disgust and surprise are combined in another expression, which is not a blend of the two messages, but produces a new message. Figure 28 shows the surprise brow/forehead and the disgust lower face, including the lower eyelid. Patricia's expression also includes an upper-eyelid droop, and her mouth is the contempt-disgust blend from Figure 26. John's expression shows a disgust lower face not shown before, where the upper lip and cheeks are raised, with slight nose-wrinkling, a raising and slight forward movement of the lower lip, and no lowering of the eyebrow. This lower face of John's is a variation of the lower face shown in Figure 23B by Patricia. These faces in Figure 28 convey disbelief. Compare this figure with Figure 5B, which shows the surprise brows and the rest of the face neutral, which had the message of questioning. By adding the disgust mouth, as in Figure 28, the message changes to disbelief, incredulity, skepticism. Frequently, such a facial expression is accompanied by back and forth lateral movements of the head.

Disgust can also blend with fear. In Figure 29 John shows fear (29A), disgust (29B), and a blend of disgust (lower face and lower eyelid) and fear (29C) (brow/forehead and upper eyelid). This blend has the meaning of dreading something disgusting.

Figure 29

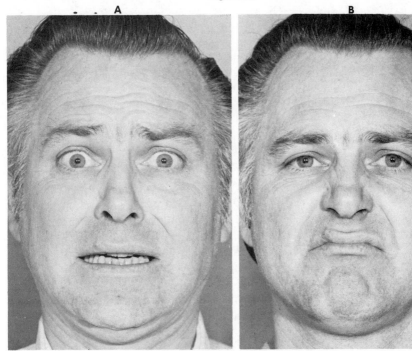

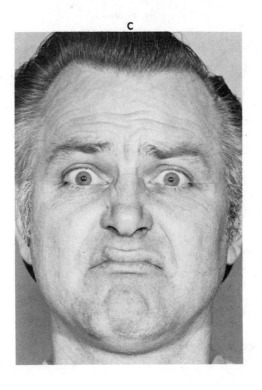

Most often, disgust blends with anger. This will be shown in the next chapter. Disgust-happiness and disgust-sadness blends will be shown in the chapters that explain those emotions.

Review

Disgust is shown primarily in the lower face and in the lower eyelid (Figure 30).

—The upper lip is raised.
—The lower lip is also raised and pushed up to the upper lip, or is lowered and slightly protruding.
—The nose is wrinkled.
—The cheeks are raised.
—Lines show below the lower lid, and the lid is pushed up but not tense.
—The brow is lowered, lowering the upper lid.

Figure 30

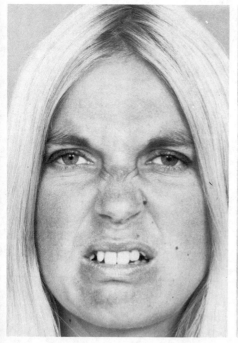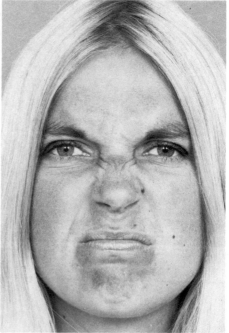

making faces

With disgust you cannot make the variations in facial expression by changing one part of the face, as you were able to do with fear and surprise. The reason for this is the connectedness across facial areas of the muscle movements involved in disgust.

The muscles that raise the upper lip also raise the cheek, and bag and fold the skin under the eyelids. Therefore, putting the B piece on the faces in Figure 30 would create something which anatomically can't occur. The eyes shown in B could not look that way if the mouth area looked the way it does in Figure 30.

The muscles responsible for wrinkling the nose also raise the cheek, slightly raise the lower lip, and bag and fold the skin under the lower eyelids. Therefore, putting the D piece on the faces in Figure 30 would create something which anatomically can't occur. If the nose is as wrinkled as it is in that figure, the upper lip would have to be raised and the tip of the nose changed in the configuration.

The muscles that lower the brow also lower the upper eyelid, narrowing the eye. Therefore, if you put the A piece on Figure 30 it would create something odd. The picture would still show the lowered eyelid even though you had removed the lowered brow.

7

anger

Anger is probably the most dangerous emotion. When angry, you are most likely to hurt others purposefully. If you know that someone is angry, if you comprehend what made him angry, then his attack is understandable even if you condemn his failure to control himself. It is the person who attacks without known provocation—who doesn't seem to have been angry—whom you judge as bizarre or crazy. Part of the experience of anger is the risk of losing control. When a person says he was angry, that often seems to explain why he did something he now regrets. "I know I shouldn't have said that to him (hit him), but I was furious; I lost my head." Children are specifically taught not to attack their parents or other adults physically when they are angry. They may even be taught to control any visible sign of anger. Boys and girls are usually trained differently about anger, girls being taught not to show anger toward anyone, while boys are encouraged to express anger toward their peers if provoked. Adults are known by how they manage the feeling of anger—"slow-burner," "short-fused," "explosive," "hothead," "cool," etc.

Anger can be aroused in a number of different ways. Frustration resulting from interference with your activity or the pursuit of your goals is one route. The frustration may be specific to a task you are engaged in or more generally to a path or direction in your life. Your anger will be more likely and more intense if you believe that the agent of the interference acted arbitrarily, unfairly, or spitefully. If a person wants to frustrate you, or frustrates you simply because he fails to consider how his actions might affect your activity, you are more likely to be angry than if you think he has no choice. The frustrating obstacle need not be a person. You can become angry at an object or natural event that frustrates you, although you may feel a bit embarrassed or less justified in your anger.

Presumably, your course of action when you are angry because of frustration is to remove the obstacle by a physical or verbal attack. Of course, the frustrator may be more powerful than you are and unconcerned with your protestations. Yet anger may still be aroused and made manifest directly to him—you may curse him, beat him, etc. Or you may manifest your anger indirectly, shouting and cursing the frustrator when he is not around to punish you for your anger. You may express your anger symbolically, by attacking something that represents him, or by displacing your anger onto a safer or more convenient target, a scapegoat.

A second major provocation to anger is a physical threat. If the person threatening injury is insignificant and obviously unable to hurt you, you are more likely to feel contempt than anger. If the person threatening injury is obviously much more powerful than you are, you will probably feel fear rather than anger. Even if the match is fairly equal, you may well experience a blend of anger and fear. The course of action when anger is aroused by a threat of physical injury may be to attack and fight, to warn verbally or bluff, or to flee. Even in flight, though you are presumably afraid, you may still also continue to feel anger.

A third major source of anger is someone's action or statement which causes you to feel psychologically, rather than physically, hurt. An insult, a rejection, an action which shows disregard for your feelings, may anger you. You must care in some way about the person who psychologically hurts you in order to feel hurt and angry about it. An insult from someone you have little regard for, a rejection by someone whom you would never consider as friend or lover, may at best call forth contempt or surprise. At the other extreme, if the hurt comes from someone you care greatly about, you may feel sadness instead of or in addition to anger. In some instances, you may care so much about the person who has hurt you, or be so unable to be angry with him (or with anyone), that you rationalize his hurtful acts by finding some basis in your own actions for his hurtful behavior; you then feel guilty rather than angry. Put in other terms, you become angry with yourself rather than with the one who hurt you. Again, as with frustration, if the person who hurts you appears to have done so deliberately, you are more likely to be angry with him than if the hurt seems accidental or otherwise out of his control.

A fourth major type of anger is occasioned by observing someone do something which violates your dearly held moral values. If someone treats another person in a manner you consider immoral you may become angry even though you are not directly affected. An obvious example is the anger you may feel when observing an adult punish a child in a fashion you consider too severe. If you hold different moral values what you perceive as an adult's leniency toward a child may anger you. The victim need not be as helpless as is a child in order for you to be angered. The husband who leaves his wife, or vice versa, may anger you, if you believe that marriage is "until death us do part." Even if wealthy you may be angered by the economic exploitation of certain groups in your society, or by the government pampering wastrels. Moral anger is often self-righteous, although we tend to apply that term only if we disagree with the moral value held by the angered person. Anger about the suffering of others, anger felt because our moral values are being violated, is a very important motive for social and political acts. Such anger in addition to other factors may motivate attempts to change society, whether it be by social reform, prayer, assassination, or terrorism.

Two other events that can cause anger are related but probably less important than the ones discussed so far. A person's failure to meet your expectations may arouse your anger. His failure need not directly hurt you; in fact it might not be directed at you per se. Most commonly this is a parental reaction to a child. Your impatience and irritation with his failure to follow instructions or otherwise meet your expectations need not require that the person hurt you by his failure to comply; it is the failure to meet expectations itself that is angering.

Another cause of anger is another person's anger directed at you. Some people characteristically reciprocate anger. This may be particularly pronounced if there is no apparent basis for the other's anger at you, or if his anger seems in your evaluation not to be justified. Anger which in your view is not as righteous as it is in his can make you quite angry.

These are only a few of the almost infinite number of causes of anger. Depending upon the life history of the individual, anything can elicit anger.

The experience of anger very often includes certain sensations. In his own account of the physiology of anger, Darwin quoted Shakespeare:

> But when the blast of war blows in our ears,
> Then imitate the action of the tiger:
> Stiffen the sinews, summon up the blood,
> Then lend the eye a terrible aspect;
> Now set the teeth, and stretch the nostril wide,
> Hold hard the breath, and bend up every spirit
> To his full height! On, on, you noblest English.

> (*Henry V,* Act 3, sc.l.)

Blood pressure increases, the face may redden, the veins on the forehead and neck may become more apparent. Breathing changes, the body may become more erect, the muscles tense, and there may be a slight movement forward toward the offender.

In intense anger or rage, it may be impossible to stay still, the impulse to strike may be so very great. Although attack, or fighting, may be a common part of the angry response, it need not occur at all. A furious person may only use words; he may shout and scream, or be more controlled and only say nasty things, or be even more controlled and not betray his anger in his words or voice. Some people habitually turn anger inward upon themselves and at the most make a joke at the expense of the anger-provoking person or at their own expense. Theories about the basis of certain psychosomatic disorders claim that certain physical illnesses occur among people who cannot express anger, who victimize themselves rather than becoming angry at those who provoke them. Currently, a lot of attention is directed to people who supposedly can't express anger, and various therapeutic and quasi-therapeutic enterprises focus specifically on teaching people how to express their anger and how to tolerate the anger of others.

Anger varies in intensity, from slight irritation or annoyance to rage or fury. Anger may build gradually, starting with irritation and slowly accumulating, or it may occur suddenly, full-blown. People differ not only in terms of what makes them angry or what they do when they are angry but also in terms of how long it takes them to become angry. Some people have short fuses, and are known for exploding in anger, rarely going through the annoyance stage no matter what the provocation. Others may rarely be aware of feeling more than annoyance; no matter what the provocation they never become really angry, at least in their view of themselves. People also differ in how long they remain angry once the provocation has passed. Some people appear to stop being angry quickly, while others characteristically experience lingering feelings of anger. It may take such people hours to get over being angry, particularly if what made them angry stopped before they had a chance to show their anger completely.

Anger can blend with any of the other emotions. We have already discussed occasions on which a person may feel anger-fear, anger-sadness, or anger-disgust. A person may also feel angry and surprised, or angry and happy at the same time, showing scorn or smugness.

Some people take considerable pleasure in the experience of being angry. They enjoy argument. Hostile exchanges and verbal attacks are not only exciting to them but are the source of satisfaction. People may even enjoy the physical exchange of blows in a knock-down drag-out physical fight. Intimacy can be established or reestablished by a vigorous angry exchange between two people. Certain married couples are known for their repetitive pattern of near-violent or even violent fights, followed immediately by sexual passion and intimacy. Some feelings of sexual excitement may occur with anger; it is not known whether this is common or peculiar to sadism. Certainly many people experience a positive feeling of relief after anger, if only because the anger is over, the threat or obstacle removed. But that is not the same as actually enjoying being angry during the experience of anger.

Enjoyment of anger is far from the only affective pattern in regard to this emotion. Many people become quite upset with themselves if they become angry; they try never to allow themselves to feel anger or show it. Never becoming angry may become an explicit part of their life philosophy or life work. People may be afraid of feeling angry. They may become sad, ashamed, or disgusted with themselves if they ever feel or show anger. Such people are usually concerned about losing control over impulses to attack. Their concern may be justified, or they may exaggerate the harm they can do or have done.

The Appearance of Anger

Although there are distinctive changes in each of the three facial areas during anger, unless changes occur in all three areas it is not clear whether or not a person is actually angry. The eyebrows are lowered and drawn together, the eyelids are tensed, and the eye appears to stare in a hard fashion. The lips are either tightly pressed together or parted in a square shape.

the anger brow

The eyebrows are drawn down and together. Figure 31 shows the anger brow at the left and the fear brow on the right. In both the anger and fear brows, the inner corners of the eyebrows are drawn together. But in anger the brow is also lowered, while in fear the brow is raised. In anger the brow may actually appear to be angled downward or just to be lowered in a flat fashion. The drawing together of the inner corners of the eyebrow usually produces vertical wrinkles between the eyebrows (1). No horizontal wrinkles will appear in the forehead in anger, and if there is any trace of such lines, they are the permanent wrinkles of the face (2).

Figure 31

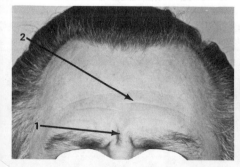 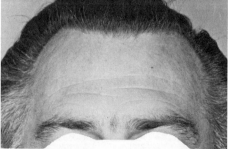

In anger the lowered, drawn-together eyebrow is usually accompanied by the anger eye and the anger mouth, but sometimes the anger brow may appear with the rest of the face uninvolved or neutral. When this happens the facial expression may or may not signify anger. In Figure 32 both John and Patricia show the anger brow with the rest of the face uninvolved on the left, a neutral face in the middle, and for comparison the fear brow with the rest of the face uninvolved on the right. Although the facial expression on the right clearly looks worried or apprehensive (as discussed in Chapter 5), the face on the left, showing the drawn-together and lowered brow, may have any of the following meanings:

—The person is angry but is trying to control or conceal any sign of anger.

—The person is slightly annoyed, or anger is in the beginning stage.

—The person is in a serious mood.

—The person is concentrating or focusing on something intently.

—If it is a momentary change, in which the anger brow appears for just a moment and then returns to a neutral position, it can be another conversational punctuator, accenting a particular word or phrase.

the anger eyes/lids

In anger the eyelids are tensed, and the eye appears to stare out in a penetrating or hard fashion. In Figure 33 Patricia and John show the two types of anger eyes, the narrower version on the left and the wider version on the right. In all four pictures the lower eyelid is tensed, but it is raised more in one type of anger eye (A) than in the other (B). With both types of anger eyes, the upper eyelid appears to be lowered. The anger eyes/lids shown in Figure 33 cannot occur without the involvement of the brow, because the lowered brow is responsible for the narrowing of the upper part of the eye, pushing against the upper eyelid. The lower eyelid could be tense and raised, and the hard, fixed stare could occur alone, but its meaning would be ambiguous. Is the person slightly angry? Is the person controlling the appearance of anger? Is the person having trouble focusing? Is the person concentrating, determined, serious? Even with both the brow/forehead and eye/lid involvement (two facial areas, as shown in Figure 33), there is the same ambiguity about what the expression means. It might have any of the meanings just listed.

the anger mouth

There are two basic types of anger mouth. In Figure 34 Patricia shows two examples of the closed, lip-pressed-against-lip mouth on the top, and of the open, square mouth on the bottom. The lip-pressed-against-lip mouth occurs in two quite different kinds of anger. It occurs when the person is

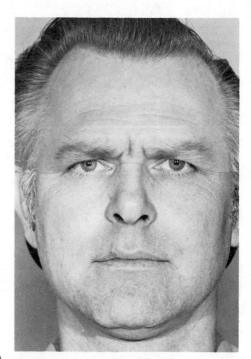

Figure 32

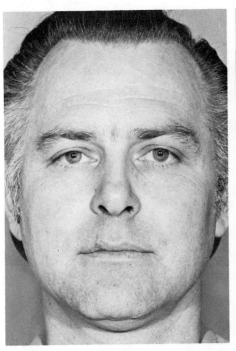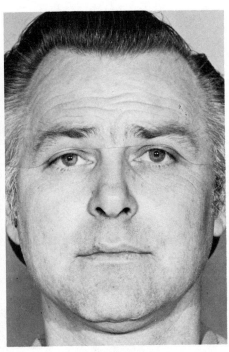
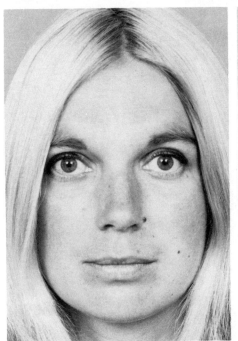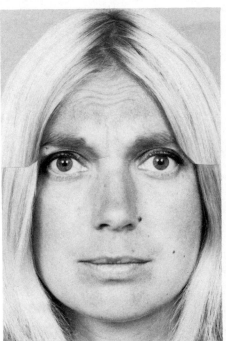

Figure 33

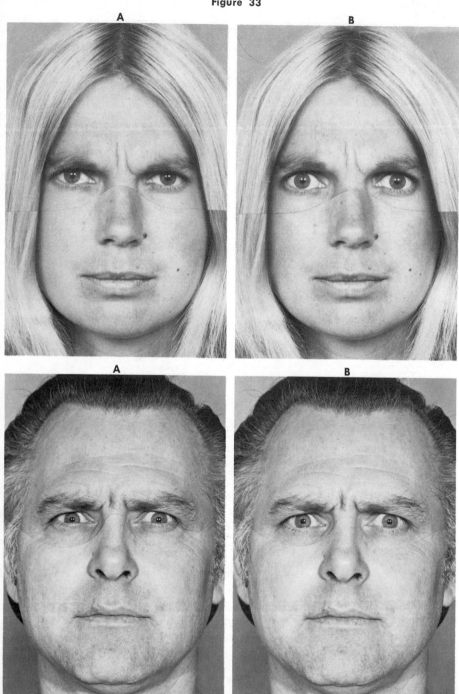

engaging in some form of physical violence, bodily attacking another person. And it occurs when the person is attempting to control a verbal, shouting anger, and presses the lips together in an attempt to keep from shouting or saying something hostile. The open-mouthed anger occurs during speech, when the person may be shouting or verbally expressing anger.

Typically these angry mouths appear with the angry eyes and brow, but they can appear with the rest of the face uninvolved. The message, however, is ambiguous, just as it is if anger is shown only in the brows or only

Figure 34

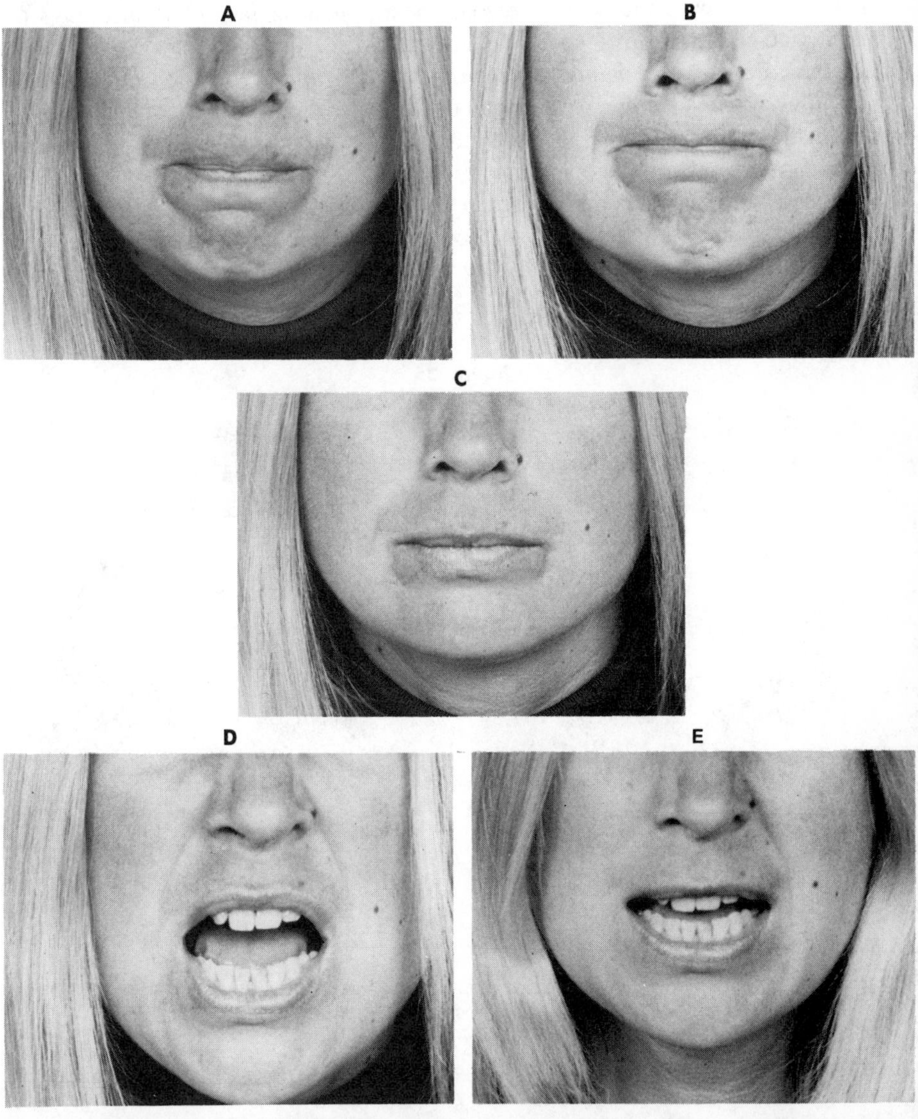

in the eyelids. If anger is shown only in the mouth, the lip-pressed-against-lip mouth may signify slight anger, controlled anger, physical exertion (such as lifting a heavy object), or concentration. The open, square mouth is also ambiguous if the rest of the face is uninvolved, for it may be occurring with nonangry shouting (yelling at a baseball game) or certain speech sounds.

two facial areas

In Figure 33 we showed that if anger is apparent in just two facial areas, the brows and eyelids, the message is ambiguous. The same is true if the anger is shown in the two areas of the mouth and eyelid. Figure 35 shows composite faces in which anger is registered in the lower face and lower eyelid, with the brow/forehead from a neutral face. The meanings of these facial expressions could be any of those just mentioned. *The facial signals for anger are ambiguous unless there is some registration of the anger in all three facial areas.* The anger facial expression is different in this way from the expressions of the emotions we have discussed so far. Surprise or fear can be shown unambiguously in the brows/eyes or the eyes/mouth. Disgust can be shown unambiguously in the mouth/eyes. In subsequent chapters on sadness and happiness you will see that these emotions can also be shown in an unambiguous fashion with only two areas of the face involved. It is only

Figure 35

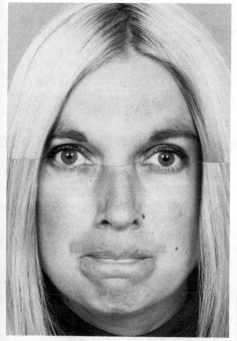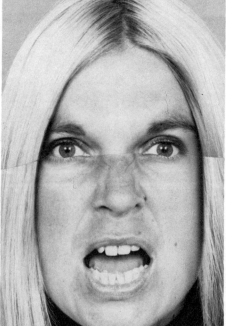

with anger that there is ambiguity if the signals are limited to only two areas of the face. The ambiguity in these two-way angers can be reduced by the tone of voice, body posture, hand movements, or words spoken, as well as by the context in which the expression occurs. If you were to see the expression shown in Figure 35 or Figure 33 when Patricia was denying that she was annoyed, clenching her fists—or were shown this expression right after you told her something you expected she would not like—you would be likely to be correct in judging her angry. Some people may have a tendency to show anger primarily in one or another facial area when they are controlling their anger. When that is so, those who know them well—members of their family or close friends—may learn something about them and the expression (as shown in Figures 35 or 33) which, while ambiguous for most people, would not be ambiguous to an intimate.

The ambiguity of anger when it is shown in only two facial areas can be demonstrated in another set of photographs in which a slightly different anger expression is shown in the eyelids. In Figure 36A the eye appears to be bulging out and the lower lid is tense, but not as tense as in Figure 33. If this occurs with the brow lowered but the mouth uninvolved, as shown in 36A, the message is ambiguous. Patricia might be experiencing controlled anger, slight anger, intent concentration, or determination. If a slight tension is added to the lower face, then the expression loses its ambiguity. On the right 36B shows the brows and eyes are the same as in 36A, but there is a slight tension in the upper lip, a slight tension in the corners of the lips and protrusion in the lower lip, and slight nostril dilation. Figure 36B is important also in showing that there need not be extreme signs of anger in all three facial areas as long as there is some registration in each. The brow/forehead in Figure 36B shows only part of the anger signal. The brow is lowered but not drawn together, and we have just outlined how mild the tension is in the lower face. Together these partial signs in the brow/forehead and lower face, with the tensed lower eyelid and bulging eye, are sufficient to signal anger.

full anger expressions

In Figure 37 Patricia shows two types of anger eyes/lids with the two types of anger mouth. Comparing the top with the bottom pictures, one sees the same eyes/lids but different mouths. Comparing the left with the right pictures, one sees the same mouth but different eyes.

As we have already explained, the two types of mouth in anger are related to what the person is doing. The closed-mouth anger shown in the top pictures can occur as the person engages in physical violence, or if the person tries to squelch an impulse to shout. What is occurring in the pictures shown at the bottom is the shouting or verbal anger. The more open-anger eye in the pictures on the right makes the message slightly more emphatic.

Figure 36

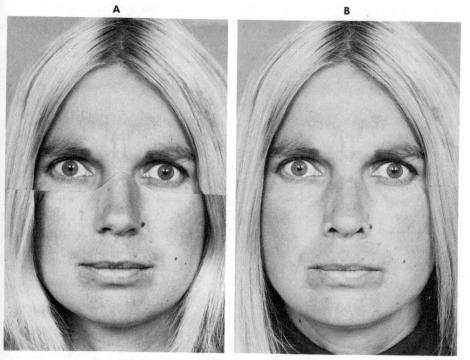

Figure 37

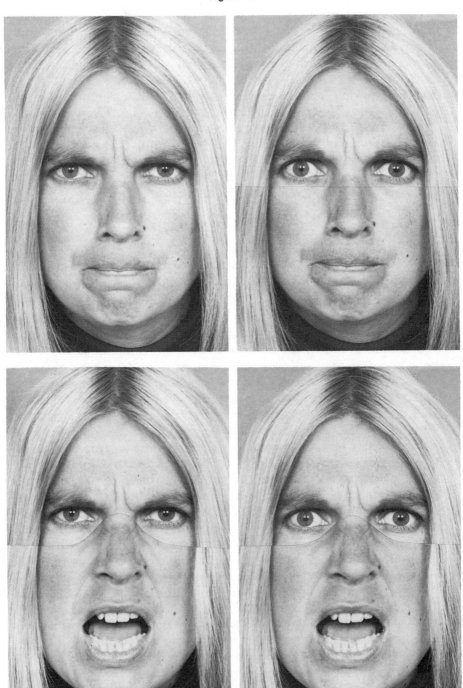

intensity of anger

The intensity of the anger expression can be manifest in how much tension there is in the eyelids or how much bulge in the eye. It can also be shown in how tightly the lips are pressed together. In Figure 37 the lip-presses are severe enough to cause a bulge below the lower lip and a wrinkling in the chin. In less intense anger the lip-press would be less severe, the bulge and chin-wrinkling less apparent or not visible. This is shown in Figure 36B. Similarly, how wide open the mouth is in the open-mouth anger expression is also related to intensity. Less intense anger can also be shown in only one part of the face, or in only two parts of the face, as in Figures 33 or 35. But, as we warned earlier, here it is not clear whether the person is just slightly angry, quite angry but controlling the appearance of anger, or not angry but concentrating, determined, or perplexed.

anger blends

The blend expressions shown in previous chapters were accomplished by the two blended emotions registering in different areas of the face. Even though limited to only part of the face, each of the blended emotions was still conveyed in the total message. With anger, however, unless the expression is registered in all three areas of the face, the message becomes ambiguous. One consequence of this is that those anger blends in which one or two facial areas register another emotion usually result in the anger message being overwhelmed by the other emotion in the blend. (Another consequence of this is that anger is easily masked—only one facial area need be controlled or covered to reduce certainty about the anger message.) You will see some examples of these blends in which the anger message is almost lost. There are two exceptions for which the anger message remains salient. First, in disgust-anger blends, the anger part of the message is retained. This may be because disgust and anger blend so frequently, or because of similarities in facial appearance and situational context between these two emotions. The second exception is that the blend may be accomplished by a different technique. A blend need not require that different facial areas show the different emotions. It can also be achieved by blending the appearance of the two emotions within each area of the face. Because the anger message is registered in all three facial areas with this type of blend, the anger message is by no means lost or swamped by the other emotion. Figure 38 shows such a blend.

Probably the most common blend for anger is with disgust. In Figure 38C Patricia shows an anger-disgust blend in which the two emotions are mixed within each facial area. It seems to say, "How dare you show me such a disgusting thing!" This figure also shows an anger expression (38A) and a disgust expression (38B) for comparison. Inspect the mouth in 38C. It is both a lip-press as in anger and an upper-lip raise as in disgust. The nose is wrinkled

Figure 38

A

B

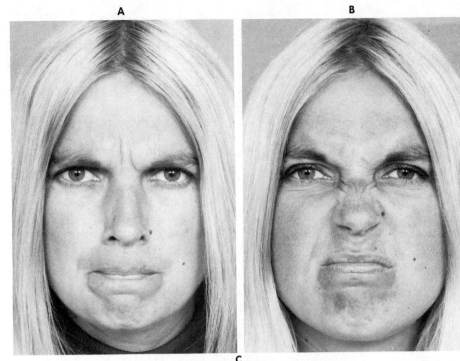

C

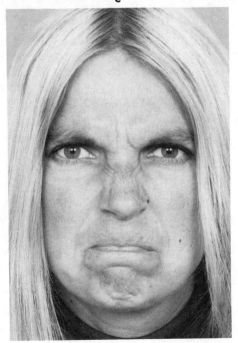

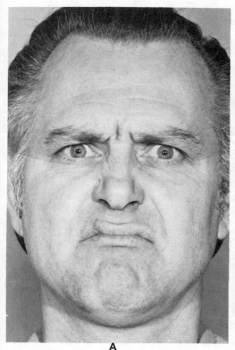 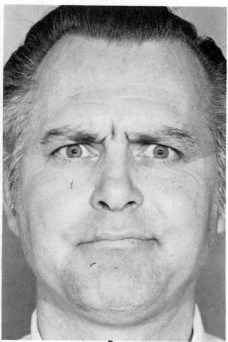

A   B

Figure 39

as in disgust. The lower eyelids have some of the tension of the anger expression but also the bagging and folding beneath the lid characteristic of disgust, which is caused by the nose-wrinkling and the raising of the cheeks. The upper eyelid appears lowered and tense, a change that can occur with either anger or disgust. But the lowered brow is intermediate between anger and disgust—the brows are only partially drawn together.

In Figure 39 John shows two other anger-disgust blends, in which the blending is accomplished by separate facial areas rather than mixing within facial areas. In 39A anger is registered in the brows and eyes and disgust in the mouth. In 39B, John shows a contempt-anger blend, with contempt in the mouth and anger in the eyes and brow.

It is possible to be surprised and angry at the same moment. Suppose John was already angry, and some new unexpected anger-provoking event happened. In Figure 40 John shows an anger-surprise blend, with surprise in the mouth and anger in the brow and eyes. Notice, however, that the surprise element—the shock—is the dominant message. It is not certain that he is also angry. This facial expression could just as well occur with perplexed surprise (remember, the lowered drawn-together brow had perplexity as one of its meanings).

Many provocations or threats may inspire both fear and anger, and the two may be blended for quite a period of time, as the person attempts

Figure 40

to cope with the situation. Figure 41 shows two such anger-fear blends. In 41B and 41C fear is shown in the mouth and anger in the brows and eyes. Again note that the anger part of the blend message is not dominant, but quite weak compared with the fear message. In fact, these two facial expressions, 41B and 41C could occur when there was no anger at all, but instead perplexed fear, or fear in which the person was concentrating. Patricia's expression in 41A has been included because it shows a combination of anger and fear elements (fear brows and eyes and anger mouth), but it is one which we doubt is an actual blend. It is more likely that this combination would occur if Patricia were afraid and attempting to keep from screaming, pressing her lips together in an attempt to control her fear.

Anger can also blend with happiness (Chapter 8) and with sadness (Chapter 9).

Review

Anger is manifested in each of the three facial areas (Figure 42).

—The brows are lowered and drawn together.
—Vertical lines appear between the brows.
—The lower lid is tensed and may or may not be raised.

Figure 41

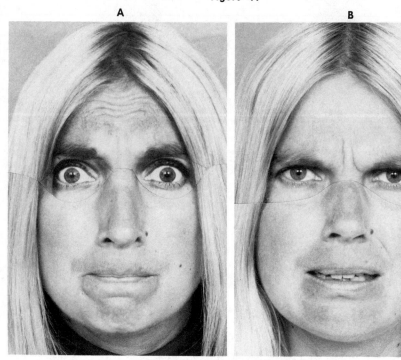

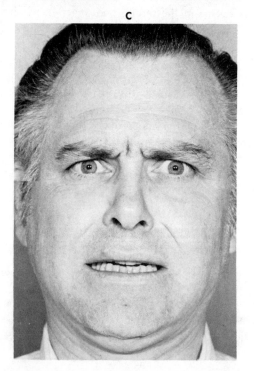

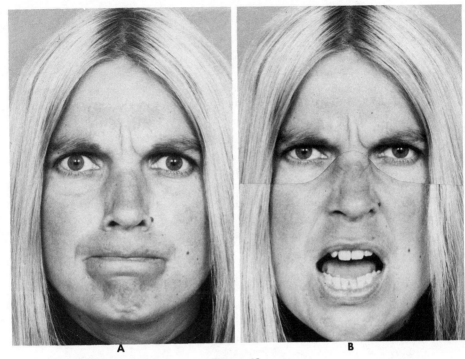

Figure 42

—The upper lid is tense and may or may not be lowered by the action of the brow.

—The eyes have a hard stare and may have a bulging appearance.

—The lips are in either of two basic positions: pressed firmly together, with the corners straight or down; or open, tensed in a squarish shape as if shouting.

—The nostrils may be dilated, but this is not essential to the anger facial expression and may also occur in sadness.

—There is ambiguity unless anger is registered in all three facial areas.

making faces

In these exercises you will be able to make the angry faces become ambiguous.

1. Put the A piece over each of the faces in Figure 42. You have made the same face as in Figure 35, which could be anger or any of the other meanings discussed.

2. Put B over each of the faces in Figure 42. You have created an expression that wasn't shown before, in which anger is registered in just the mouth. This could be controlled anger or slight anger; or it could be muscular exertion, concentration, shouting to someone, or speech.

3. Put C over the faces in Figure 42. This is the same as shown in Figure 32. Again the message is ambiguous: controlled or slight anger, concentration, determination, etc.

4. Put D over the faces in Figure 42. This is the same as in Figure 33 and again is ambiguous, with the same choice in messages as listed just above.

flashing faces

Check the instructions for Flashing Faces on pages 63-64. Now, you can add disgust and anger faces, and blends of anger, disgust, fear and surprise. First practice the anger, disgust and blends of these two emotions listed below. When you have them perfect, add the list of fear and surprise pictures you practiced earlier (page 64). Practice until you are able to get them all correct.

List of Faces for Flashing Faces, Practice Two:

Figure Number:	Answers:
24A	Full Face Disgust
24B	Full Face Disgust
25A	Contempt
25B	Contempt
25C	Contempt
27C	Surprise-Disgust Blend or Emphatic Disgust
28, left photo	Disbelief
28, right photo	Disbelief
29C	Fear-Disgust Blend
33A, lower left photo	Controlled, Slight Anger or Perplexed, Concentrating etc.
33B, upper right photo	Slight Anger, Controlled Anger, Concentrating etc.
36B	Controlled or Slight Anger
37, upper right photo	Full Face Anger
37, lower left photo	Full Face Anger
38C	Anger-Disgust Blend
39A	Anger-Disgust Blend
39B	Anger-Contempt Blend
41B	Fear-Anger Blend or Perplexed Fear

8

happiness

Happiness is the emotion most people want to experience. You like being happy. It feels good. You choose situations, if you can, in which you will experience happiness. You may organize your life in order to increase your happy experiences. Happiness is a positive emotion. By comparison fear, anger, disgust, and sadness are negative emotions, and most people do not enjoy them. Surprise is neither positive nor negative. In order to understand the experience of happiness, we need to distinguish it from two closely related states which often occur with happiness—pleasure and excitement.

Although our language assigns almost synonymous meanings to the words *pleasure, happiness,* and *enjoyment,* here we want to restrict the term pleasure to refer solely to positive *physical sensations.* This pleasure is the opposite of the physical sensation of pain. Pain hurts, while pleasure is intrinsically good or rewarding in the way it feels. You value, appreciate, and prefer pleasurable sensations. We do not know all the ways that pleasure sensations can be evoked. Certainly tactile stimulation and taste can bring on pleasurable sensations, and so can some sounds and sights. Usually you feel happy when you experience pleasurable sensations, unless you have been punished for having such sensations and feel guilty about them or about your way of obtaining pleasure. Often you feel happy in anticipation of an event which you know will cause pleasurable sensations, or happy, in a contented way, afterward. But you do not need to experience pleasurable sensations to be happy. There are other routes to happiness which don't involve pleasurable sensations.

Excitement is considered by the psychologist Silvan Tomkins to be a primary emotion, different from but equal in importance to surprise, anger, fear, disgust, sadness, and happiness. We agree, but have chosen not to discuss this emotion for two reasons. There is not yet sufficient evidence that its appearance is universal, although we believe that to be the case. Also, it would be hard to show the appearance of this emotion in still photographs; the facial signs are subtle. We will describe excitement only sufficiently to distinguish it from happiness.

Excitement is the opposite of boredom. You become excited when something arouses your interest. Often it is something novel. If it is familiar, it is not merely repetitive. You become attentive, involved, and quite aroused with what has excited you. In boredom, nothing holds your attention, nothing seems to be happening, nothing is new, nothing interests you. You may be happy at the prospect of something exciting, particularly if it is going to relieve a bored state; and often, you are happy after excitement. But that is only one kind of happiness, for you can be happy without excitement as an accompaniment. It is also quite possible to be excited and in no way happy; excitement can blend instead with fear, as in a terrorized state, or with anger, as in a state of fury.

In sexual experiences you can and usually do experience all three states—pleasure from the erotic sensations prior to and during orgasm, excitement prior to orgasm, and happiness in anticipation of the sexual encounter and happy contentment subsequent to the drop in excitement following orgasm. Though this is the likely combination, it is not a necessary one. The emotion subsequent to orgasm may be disgust or sadness. Or during the excitement-pleasure phase, you might experience fear or disgust, and this may end the excitement and abort the sexual encounter. Or anger may coincide with sexual arousal, excitement, and pleasure, and may or may not interrupt the encounter.

Many people think of happiness as either pleasure or excitement or both, failing to distinguish among these experiences. Pleasure and excitement are separate experiences which often involve happiness, and thus can be considered two possible routes to happy feelings. Each of these routes involves a somewhat differently colored happy experience, so that we can speak of pleasure-happiness or excitement-happiness. The third route is relief-happiness.

When pain stops, you are usually happy. Similarly, when hunger or thirst is met, you are happy. The same is usually true for the negative emotions. When you are no longer afraid, when anger ends, when the disgust is over, when the sadness lifts, commonly you feel happy. It is the happiness of relief. It may also involve happiness in accomplishment, if it is by your own efforts that the experience of the negative emotion or sensation is terminated. As with pleasure and excitement, some people fail to distinguish relief from happiness. For some people it is the only kind of happiness they experience often. Their lives are primarily organized to obtain relief rather than to experience pleasure or excitement. Relief-happiness is a somewhat different experience—the sensations, the images, the likely actions, the general feelings registered—from pleasure-happiness, excitement-happiness, or happiness reached by the fourth route.

The fourth type of happiness involves the self-concept. Something happens that enhances your view of yourself, something that affirms or further elaborates a favorable self-concept. If you find that somebody likes you, you will often feel happy—not because you expect the person to cause pleasurable physical sensations or sexual excitement, but because being liked makes you feel good about yourself. If someone tells you that you have done a good job at something, you feel happy. Praise, friendship, the esteem of others is rewarding and makes you feel happy. It is not the kind of happiness in which you usually will burst out laughing. It is a more contented, smiling happiness. This kind of happiness originally develops from experiences in which those who gave approval—such as parents—also physically stroked, fed, and relieved pain. As a child develops, social approval becomes rewarding in itself. As with happiness experienced by the other routes, anticipating or remembering a boost to your self-concept will produce happy feelings.

If you think of the situations and events that cause you to feel happy, you will probably find that they involve one or more of the four routes described. For example, the enjoyment you experience while engaging in a sports activity may involve excitement-happiness associated with the contest, pleasure-happiness from the movements and exertions, self-concept happiness because you are playing well, and relief-happiness because you haven't let the team down, missed a shot, or broken your neck, etc. It is not necessary to our purpose here to claim that these are the only routes to happiness. There may well be more, but we believe these four are common and important, and their description should make clear what we mean by the happiness experience.

Happiness varies not only in type, as we have discussed, but also in intensity. You can be mildly happy, and you can experience ecstasy or joy. Happiness can be shown silently or audibly. It can vary from a smile to a broad grin and, at some stage along the line, there can be chuckling as well, or laughter or, in the most extreme form, laughter with tears. The presence of laughing or chuckling does not indicate the intensity of the happiness. You can be extremely happy and not laugh; laughing or chuckling occurs with particular types of happy experiences. Play of one kind or another, in children or adults, if sufficiently exciting, will often produce the laughing type of happiness. Certain jokes can produce the laughing happiness.

Smiles, which are part of the happiness facial expression, often occur when a person is not happy. You smile to mask other emotions, or to qualify them. Smiles may comment on another emotion being shown, such as smiling after a fear expression to let the nurse know that, though afraid, you will not flee but let her take blood from your arm. Smiles may indicate submissiveness to anything unpleasant, not just to the infliction of pain. Commonly, smiling may be a submissive response to ward off or call a halt to another's attack. Smiles may also be used to make a tense situation more comfortable; by smiling you can cause the other person to smile also, because it is hard to resist returning a smile. We will discuss these uses of the happiness facial expression in Chapter 11, "Facial Deceit."

Happiness can blend with any of the other emotions. In this chapter we will show blends of happiness with surprise, anger, disgust, contempt, and fear. In the next chapter happiness-sadness blends will be shown.

In discussing each of the emotions, we have suggested that childhood experiences leave their imprint, that personality may be shown in how each emotion is experienced. We have suggested that people differ in whether they can enjoy, tolerate, or find bearable the feelings of surprise, fear, disgust or anger (and sadness, as will be described in the next chapter). The same is true with feelings of happiness. Not everyone feels happy in the same way. Not all four routes—pleasurable sensation, excitement, relief, enhancement of self-concept—are available to everyone. One route may be used more than another because of particular personality characteristics. One route may be blocked, with the person unable to experience happiness by that means. We can give only a few examples here.

A child may grow up subject to so much criticism, or with so little appreciation by others of his worth, that as an adult he hungers for praise, affirmation, and friendship. The self-concept route may be the most heavily travelled, but he may not be able to be happy for long. The praise of others may never be enough, or not be trusted as genuine. With a similar childhood that fails to build an adequate self-concept, just the opposite pattern may be evident in adult life. A person may be so discouraged that the self-concept route is not employed at all. He may be distant from others, unable to enjoy friendship, not seeking praise or reward for accomplishment.

Much has been written about people who have trouble as adults in achieving happiness in their sexual activities. Children are taught by some parents to distrust or despise the "pleasures of the body." As adults, sex for these individuals may be experienced with anxiety or guilt rather than pleasure. Other sensual experiences may similarly be devoid of pleasure, or enjoyed only at the cost of subsequent shame. A child may grow up afraid of excitement, having learned that it is dangerous to become excited—that it displeases others and is often unmanageable. Happiness is a quieter experience for such a person. Or a person may become addicted to excitement, seeking greater challenges, ever spurred on to seek happiness in excitement.

We will be concerned here only with the appearance of the face in the nonlaughing happiness expression, for when laughter occurs as well there is little problem in determining that the person is happy. Even in the silent happy expression, recognition is remarkably simple, except perhaps for some of the blends. The ease in recognizing the happy expression has been shown in studies of many different cultures.

There is a distinctive appearance in the eyelids and lower face, while the brow/forehead is not necessarily involved in the happy expression. In Figure 43, Patricia shows three happy facial expressions. In each, the corners of the lips are drawn back and slightly up. The lips may remain together in a smile (A), the lips may be parted, with the teeth and jaw together in a grin (B), or the mouth may be opened and the teeth parted in a wide grin (C). In wide-mouth grins only the upper teeth may show, or both upper and lower teeth may be exposed, or the gums, upper and/or lower, may also be shown. In chimpanzees these different types of grins have different related meanings, but there is no evidence as yet that for humans there is any common difference in the meaning of the different grins.

Patricia also shows wrinkle lines running from the nose out and down to the area beyond the corners of the mouth. These "naso-labial folds" occur partly as a result of the pulling back and up of the corners of the lips and are a characteristic sign of the happy facial expression. In addition, the cheek becomes raised when there is a pronounced smile or grin, intensifying the naso-labial folds. The skin below the lower eyelid is pushed up, and lines are formed below the eye. "Crow's-feet" wrinkling is also formed at the outer corner of the eyes. Not everyone shows crow's-feet; they become more apparent with age. In Patricia's pictures they are hidden by her hair. The more extreme the smile or grin, the more pronounced will be the naso-labial folds, the raising of the cheek, the crow's feet, and the lines under the eyes. With the wide-mouth grin, as shown in 43C, the cheek may be lifted far enough to actually narrow the eyes. In happiness there may also be a sparkle in the eyes, a glistening.

intensity

The intensity of a happy expression is primarily determined by the position of the lips, but the lip position is usually accompanied by deepening of the naso-labial fold and more pronounced lines under the lower eyelid. In 43C Patricia shows more intense happiness than in 43B—her grin is broader, the naso-labial folds more pronounced; her eyes narrower, with more lines underneath them. The expression in 43A is slightly less intense than 43B. This is not because her mouth is open in 43B and closed in 43A,

Figure 43

A

B

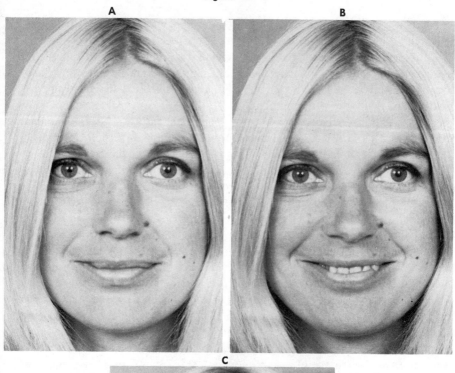

C

but because the spreading back of the corners of her lips (and the naso-labial folds) is greater in 43B than in 43A. If the drawing back of the corners of the lips and naso-labial folds is about the same, then whether the mouth is a closed smile or an open grin, the intensity is about the same. In Figure 44 John shows an example of a smile and a grin which are about the same in intensity.

The smile of happiness can be much slighter than those shown in Figures 43 and 44. In Figure 45 Patricia shows two such very slight happy smiles, with her neutral face below for comparison. Note that both of these smiles are less intense than her smile in 43A, but that the smile is there, because these pictures do look happy when compared with her neutral picture in Figure 45C. Both of Patricia's smiling faces in Figure 45 are composed of just the slight tensing and slight drawing back of the corners of the lips. This is easiest to see if you cover the rest of her face with your hand and compare just the lips in the three pictures. Note also the beginning trace of a naso-labial fold in both smiling pictures as compared to the neutral one. You can also see that her cheeks are slightly raised in the smiling pictures as compared to the neutral picture, making her face look somewhat fuller. There is no noticeable change in the lower eyelid, when the smile is

Figure 44

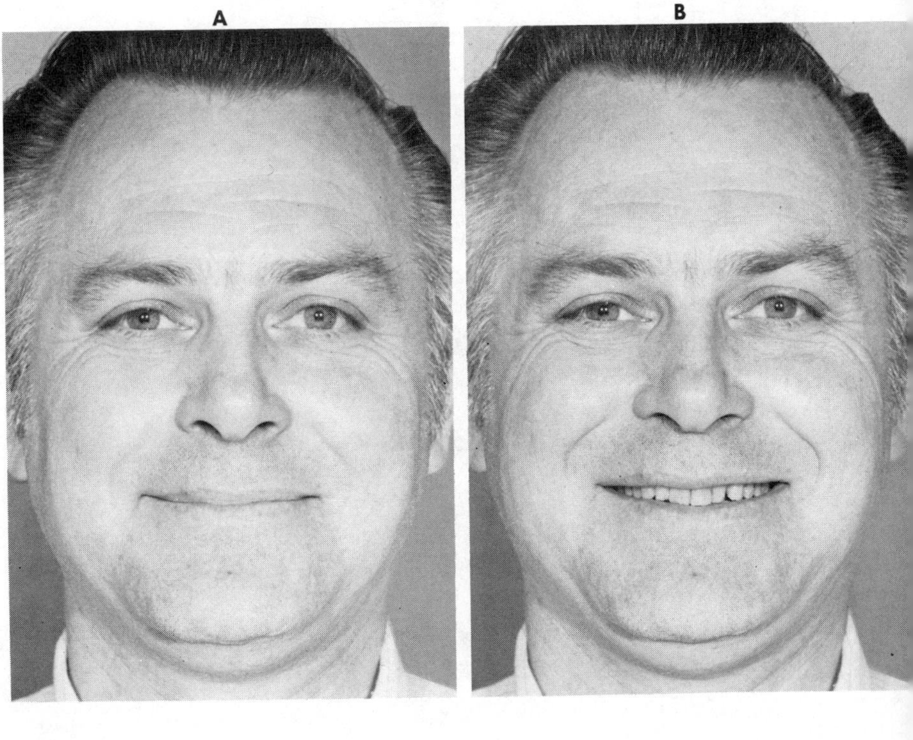

A   B

Figure 45

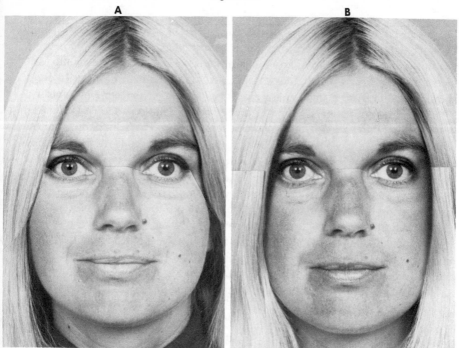

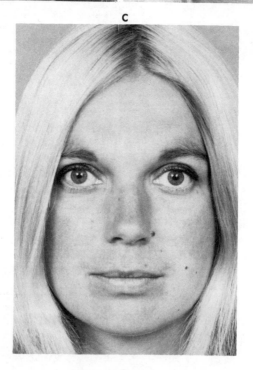

this slight. Although the eyes themselves look more happy in the smiling pic-tures than in the neutral one, this only reflects the lower face, because the eyes and brow/forehead are the same in all three pictures. The smiling ones are composites, in which the neutral eyes and forehead have been combined with the lower eyelids and mouth from the smiling photographs.

blends

Happiness often blends with surprise. Something unexpected occurs, and the evaluation of it is favorable. For example, a friend not seen for many years walks without prior warning into the restaurant where you are eating lunch. In Figure 46A Patricia shows a surprise-happy blend. Comparing it with the surprise-only picture (Figure 46B), note that the difference is solely in the lower face. In the blend expression her mouth is not only dropped open as in surprise, but the corners of her lips have begun to draw back as in a smile. This blend is accomplished by mixing elements of both surprise and happiness in the lower face. (You saw an example of another mixed blend in Figure 38.) A happy-surprise expression would only be shown for a moment, because the surprise would last only briefly. By the time she evaluated the surprising event and began to feel and show happiness, her surprise would quickly fade. In Figure 46C Patricia shows a combination of surprise and happy elements (surprise brows/forehead and eyes with happy lower face, including lower eyelid), but it is not a blend expression. She is not surprised and happy simultaneously, because the happiness is too far advanced; she is already into a grin, and if there was surprise it should have already passed. This type of facial expression will occur, however, if the person is adding an exclamatory note to a happy expression. Enthusiasm or emphasis might also be shown in this way. Or such an expression can occur in greeting, the surprise elements held to be certain that the other person realizes it is an "unexpected pleasure." In such a happy expression the raised brow and open eye might remain for a few seconds with the grin.

Happiness blends with contempt, producing a smug, scornful or superior expression. In Figure 47 John shows a contempt expression (47A), a happy expression (47B), and a blend of the two below (47C). Notice that his mouth remains in the contempt position, but the cheeks are raised and the lower eyelid wrinkled from the happy expression. The happy-contempt blend can also occur with the unilateral raised lip of contempt combined with a smiling lip.

Happiness also blends with anger. Most commonly, a smile or slight grin is used to mask anger, in which case the person looks happy, not angry. A smile or slight grin sometimes appears after an angry expression as a comment on the anger, saying essentially it is not too serious, or the person

Figure 46

A

B

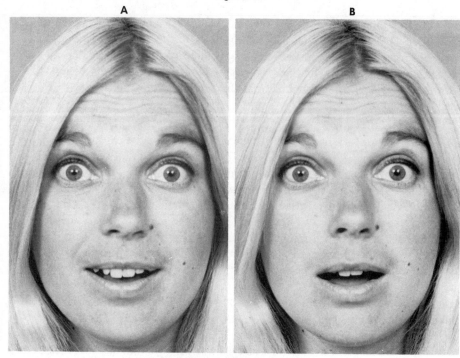

C

Figure 47

A   B

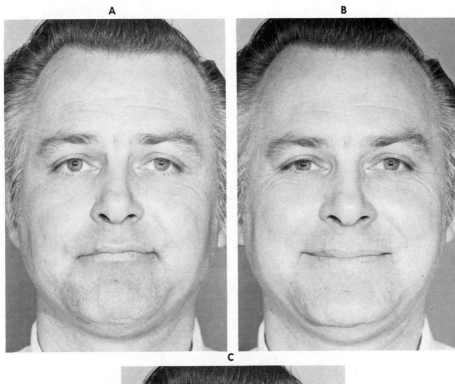

C

doesn't intend to act on his anger, or the person who is the object of the anger will be forgiven. In such an instance the smile or grin doesn't look very genuine, and is not blended with anger, but added afterward. It is possible, however, for a person to be both happy and angry at the same time, enjoying his anger, his triumph over another person. Two examples of such delight-anger are shown in Figure 48. In each case the happiness is shown in the lower face, and anger in the brow/forehead and eyelids. These are "I've gotcha" expressions.

Happiness also combines with fear. Most commonly, the expression is not a blend, but either a comment or a mask. In Figure 49 John shows a fear expression (49A), happiness (49B) and a combination of the two (49C) (smile with fear eyes and brow/forehead). This smiling fear expression might occur if John, fearing the dentist's drill, smiles for a moment as he gets into the dental chair to comment on the fact that he is going to grin and bear it. An unsuccessful attempt to mask fear could also result in this expression. It could be a genuine blend if John felt both afraid and happy—as, for example, while on a roller-coaster. The blends of happiness with sadness will be shown in the next chapter.

Figure 48

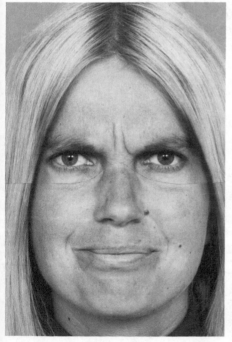

Figure 49

A

B

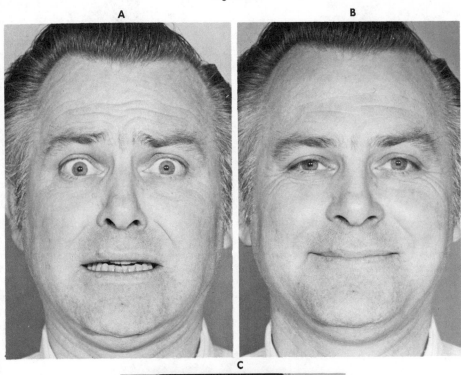

C

| A | B |

Figure 50

Happiness is shown in the lower face and lower eyelids (Figure 50).

—Corners of lips are drawn back and up.

—The mouth may or may not be parted, with teeth exposed or not.

—A wrinkle (the naso-labial fold) runs down from the nose to the outer edge beyond the lip corners.

—The cheeks are raised.

—The lower eyelid shows wrinkles below it, and may be raised but not tense.

—Crow's-feet wrinkles go outward from the outer corners of the eyes (covered by hair in Figure 50).

making faces

Because the movements around the mouth and cheeks also change the appearance of the lower eyelids, and because there is no distinctive brow/ forehead movement in happiness, you cannot make most of the faces shown in this chapter. You can, however, make a few faces that will demonstrate these points to you.

1. Put A on either of the faces in Figure 50. There is no change in the expression. Because the brows are not involved in these happy faces, covering the brow with the neutral brow in piece A has no effect.

2. Put B on 50A. It doesn't look odd, but anatomically it is not possible. If that mouth movement occurs, with those naso-labial folds, the lower eyelid must be wrinkled and lifted. Put B on 50B. It should be more obvious that this face cannot occur anatomically.

3. Put D on either of the faces in Figure 50. You have created a facial expression in which there are "smiling eyes." This look could result from a slight tensing of the eyelid and raising of the cheek, which would be difficult to note on a still photograph. Or this appearance could be this person's permanent wrinkles. In any case the happiness clues are very slight, at best.

9

sadness

The Experience of Sadness

In sadness your suffering is muted. You do not cry aloud but more silently endure your distress. Anything can make you sad, but most often you are sad about losses. Loss through death or rejection by a loved one. Loss of an opportunity or reward through your own mistaken effort, or circumstance, or another's disregard. Loss of your health, or of some part of your body through illness or accident. Sadness is rarely a brief feeling. You are usually sad for at least minutes and more typically for hours or even days.

Sadness is a passive, not an active feeling. Darwin wrote of sad persons that

> they no longer wish for action, but remain motionless and passive, or may occasionally rock themselves to and fro. The circulation becomes languid; the face pale; the muscles flaccid; the eyelids droop; the head hangs on the contracted chest; the lips, cheeks and lower jaw all sink downward from their own weight. (1965, p. 176) [1]

You suffer in sadness. It is not the suffering of physical pain; it is the suffering of loss, disappointment, or hopelessness. The suffering in sadness can be extreme, but in its extremity it is more tolerable than the suffering of fear. You can endure sadness for longer periods of time and survive.

Sadness is a variation or form of distress, which is the most general negative emotion. Distress is most easily and often aroused by physical pain.

[1] From C. Darwin, *The expression of the emotions in man and animals.* Chicago: University of Chicago Press, 1965. Reproduced by permission of the Publisher.

Loss can also call forth distress. You suffer in distress, but the suffering is loud, not quiet; the cry is audible, not muted. There is activity rather than passivity. In distress you attempt to cope with that which caused the distress. The coping may be purposefully removing the source of distress—for example, removing a tack from your heel. Often the coping in distress appears purposeless because there is little that can be done to remove the source of distress, as for example, the wailing while mourning the death of a loved one. Sadness often follows distress if the distress is prolonged or if the coping actions to remove the source of distress are unsuccessful. As distress lingers, the cries become muted, the activity decreases, the suffering is more silent. Often a memory or someone's action will restimulate the distress, and the sequence recycles—loud complaining distress followed again by sadness. The word *sadness* can also be applied when distress is controlled deliberately—when the loud, active elements are not visible, but only the more socially acceptable signs of sadness.

If your child has just been killed by an automobile, your immediate reaction will not be sadness. It will be distress or perhaps shock or anger blended with distress. The sadness will come later, hours or maybe even days later, when you are still suffering the loss but have stopped weeping and audible crying, at least for a period of time. In distress there is more of a protest against the loss; in sadness you are resigned to the loss. Grief and mourning imply the *cause* of the feeling—death of a loved one—but not whether the person is in distress or sadness. Typically there is a sequence in which distress is followed by either disbelief or sadness, which recycles back to distress as some new remembrance of the deceased or some new reminder of his death occurs, and over and over again the sequence repeats. As time elapses, all that may remain are periods of sadness, perhaps lasting over months or years.

In a romantic loss the pattern is similar. The rejected lover initially shows distress. There will be crying and protestation, perhaps also shock and anger, or some combination of these. Sadness comes later, perhaps followed by disbelief in the rejection, and a recycling of the whole suffering experience. If the rejected lover never showed distress—if there was never any crying or agitation—you would suspect that this is a highly controlled person, or someone who doesn't care that much about the lost lover, or a person exhibiting stereotypical American masculine behavior. It is not proper for men to show distress in public, even at funerals; they are limited to sadness. The cry must be inhibited, the agitated movements and the protestations held in check or shown only as anger. Although anger is often experienced with distress or sadness, it is also often used as a mask to cover distress. Interestingly, while social conventions prohibit the appearance of distress and in its place allow the show of anger for men, just the opposite is prescribed for women. Women who are following the American stereotyped demands of "femininity" will not show anger toward others openly but instead will turn anger inward upon themselves, or show distress, angry tears, or sulking.

When sadness results from controlling distress, it probably appears the same as the sadness that is the aftermath of shown distress, but the experience is likely to feel different. When you control the appearance of distress, your face may look sad, but the experience you are having, what you are aware of, the sensations, images, memories, and concerns, all are changed by the necessity to control your behavior. It doesn't feel the same as if you were crying in distress, and it doesn't feel the same as if you had been previously crying in distress and were now in the post-distress sadness.

Sadness varies in intensity from slight feelings of being "blue" or gloomy to the extreme felt during mourning. Sadness is not necessarily less intense than distress; both vary in their intensity. Because sadness is quieter, less turbulent, less vocal, less protesting than distress, it is easier on others to be in the presence of someone who is sad. But the person may feel worse in sadness than in distress, as he has become more resigned to his loss and suffering and is better able to reflect on its meaning.

Sadness can blend with any of the emotions, but most often blends with anger and fear. The death of a loved one can elicit anger as well as distress and sadness—anger at the forces responsible for the death, anger at the loved one for dying, anger at the self for being so vulnerable. And as just mentioned, anger can be exaggerated or simulated to conceal the distressed or sad expression. If you learn that your leg must be amputated, you might well feel fear of the danger and physical pain as well as distress or sadness about the impending bodily loss. Sadness can blend with disgust in a disappointed disgust or disdain. And sadness can blend with happiness in a bittersweet feeling or in a sentimental resemblance of a melancholic time from the past.

Some people enjoy the experience of sadness. There are vicarious sadness experiences which some people seek, just as others seek the pseudo-fear experience in the roller coaster. Some people purposefully make themselves sad, or find opportunities to cry by attending movies or reading novels known as tear-jerkers. Others can never show distress, and find sadness—even vicarious sadness—a noxious experience. They are considered cold, nonempathetic people who do not care about others sufficiently to be moved by their suffering or death.

The Appearance of Sadness

We have chosen to focus upon sadness rather than distress because distress is more obvious in its appearance. It is more readily understood, also, because it is typically accompanied by audible crying. Not so with sadness. In its most extreme form, there may be no facial clue to sadness other than the loss of muscle tone in the face. Such sad expressions cannot be shown in photographs. With less severe sadness, and when the person moves in transition from distress to sadness, there are distinctive facial clues. The facial expressions we will show here for such sad messages may also occur when distress is slight or just beginning.

There is a distinctive appearance in each of the three facial areas during sadness. The inner corners of the eyebrows are raised and may be drawn together. The inner corner of the upper eyelid is drawn up, and the lower eyelid may appear raised. The corners of the lips are drawn down, or the lips appear to tremble.

the sadness brow

The inner corners of the eyebrows are raised, and may be drawn together. In Figure 51 John and Patricia show the sad brow/forehead, with an otherwise neutral face on the left and a fear brow/forehead, with an otherwise neutral face on the right for comparison. In John's picture note that the inside corners of the eyebrows are raised (1) in sadness; this differs from the raising and drawing together of the *whole* eyebrow in his fear/brow forehead. Although the same difference in muscular action has occurred in the pictures of Patricia, it is much less apparent. There are two ways to see that the same thing has happened in Patricia's brow/forehead as in John's. Look at the shape of the skin under her eyebrows in 51C and compare it with 51D. Notice the triangular shape in the sad brow (2) not present in the fear brow, which results from the muscles pulling the inner corner of the eyebrow up. You can see the same effect in John's picture. Another way to observe Patricia's version of the sadness brow is to compare the total impression given by her face on the left with her face on the right. On the left the total impression is slight sadness, as compared to the slight worry on the right, even though both pictures are composites and differ only in the brow/forehead. The same differences are more obvious in the pictures of John in Figure 51.

These pictures of the sad brow/forehead in Figure 51 also show the sadness upper eyelid. We could not show the sadness brow/forehead without the upper eyelid, because the muscular movement that affects the brow in this emotion also pulls the inner corner of the upper eyelid. In the sadness pictures of John and Patricia the upper eyelid is pulled up at the inner corner or top of the lid.

Usually the sad brow/forehead (and upper eyelid) will be accompanied by the sad lower eyelid and lower face. But it can occur alone. When this is shown with the rest of the face uninvolved, the expression can mean that the person is feeling a little sad, or that the person is controlling the expression of a more intense sadness. Or when it is flashed on and off during conversa-

Figure 51

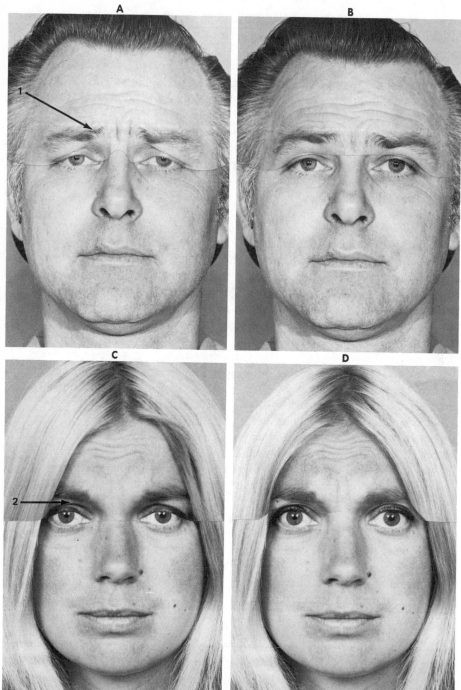

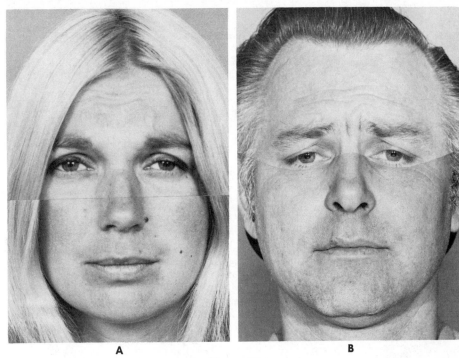

A   B

Figure 52

tion, it can punctuate a phrase or join the voice in stressing a particular word. This is an alternative to the use of the raised brow (Chapter 4, Figure 4) or the lower brow (Chapter 7, Figure 31), which also are used as "punctuators."

sadness brow/forehead and eyelids

The faces in Figure 52 differ from the sadness pictures in Figure 51 only in that the sad lower eyelid has been substituted for the neutral lower eyelid in Figure 51. Raising the lower lid increases the sadness conveyed. Patricia looks sadder in Figure 52 than she does in 51C, even though these pictures differ in only one respect—the lower eyelid.

The picture of John in Figure 52 not only has the sad lower lid but also the eyes are slightly cast down. Often in sadness the gaze is down rather than straight ahead, particularly if there is shame or guilt blended in with the sadness. There is still some element of control when the mouth is neutral, as in these pictures; but the sadness is more pronounced than in the faces shown in Figure 51.

the sad mouth

In Figure 53A and 53B Patricia shows two sadness mouths. The mouth that is most often confused with it, a disgust-contempt mouth, is shown in

Figure 53

A

B

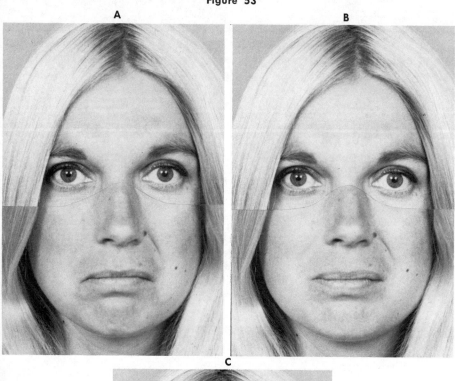

C

53C. In all three pictures the eyes and brow/forehead are neutral. In Figure 53A Patricia shows the corners of the lips down, in Figure 53B she shows the loose-lip characteristic of the mouth when it is trembling, or when the person is about to cry or is trying to withhold crying. The disgust-contempt mouth is shown in 53C to emphasize how it differs from sadness.

When sadness is shown only in the mouth (no involvement of the eyelids or forehead), the facial expression is ambiguous. This is not the case with all of the other emotions (happiness, surprise, fear, and disgust shown only in the mouth yield nonambiguous facial expressions). The expression in 53A might be a pout, but this is not certain. The message in 53B is completely ambiguous; it might be mild distress, defiance, or anything.

full-face sadness and intensity

In Figure 54 Patricia shows sadness across all three areas of the face, with each of the sadness mouths. The faces in Figure 54 are of moderate intensity. Less intense sadness is conveyed by less involvement of the different facial areas. The slightest sadness was seen in 51C. The next step of in-

Figure 54

A   B

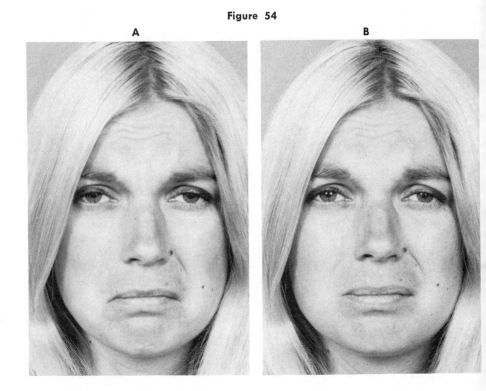

creasing intensity was in 52A. More intense sadness than that shown in Figure 54 is quite possible, but it has to do with tearing in the eyes and movements of the lips, such as trembling, which are not possible to depict in still photographs. More intense sadness might be shown by a rather blank appearance due to marked loss of muscle tone.

sadness blends

In Figure 55 John and Patricia show a blend of sadness (brow/eyelids) with fear (mouth). It might occur if Patricia, for example, saddened after a natural disaster in which she had lost her home, now is told that everyone must evacuate the area because there is a new danger; then fear or apprehension might blend with sadness. The faces shown in Figure 55 could also occur when there is distress, without crying, about actual or impending physical pain. The cry or scream might well follow soon with such a facial expression.

Figure 56C shows the blend of sadness (mouth) with anger (brow/forehead and eyes/lids), with full facial expressions of anger (56A) and sadness

Figure 55

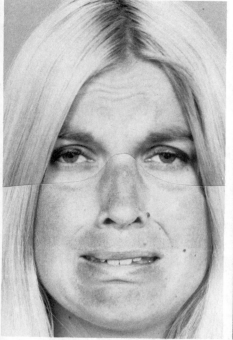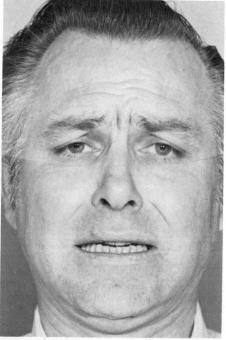

Figure 56

A

B

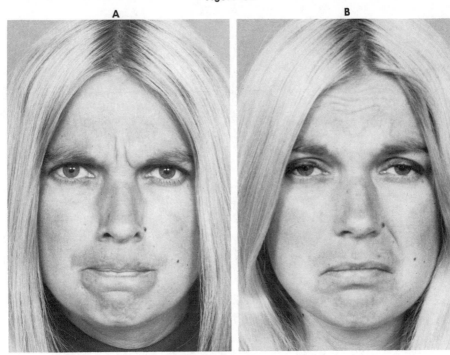

C

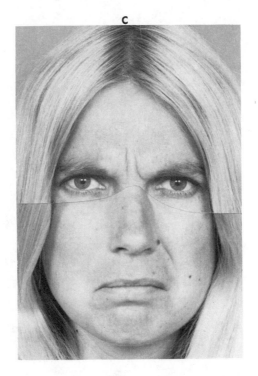

Figure 57

A

B

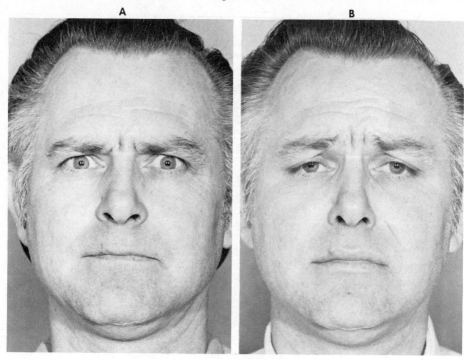

C

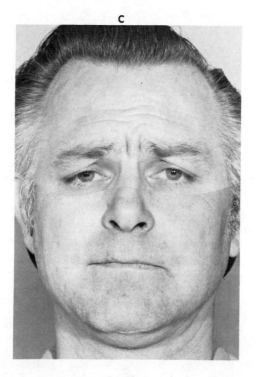

(56B) for comparison. This facial expression might occur, for example, if Patricia had just approached a reckless driver who had run over her dog. Saddened at the death of her pet, angry at the driver for his carelessness, she might blend the two feelings in this expression. Or Patricia might have been scolded by her mother. Feeling both saddened by the temporary loss of love and angry at her mother, she might blend the two in a sulky anger, or pout. In Figure 57C John shows another blend of sadness (brows/eyes) with anger (mouth), and also full anger (57A) and sadness (57B) expressions for comparison. This sadness-anger blend is most likely the result of attempting to mask or at least control the sad expression with the anger mouth. Or it could be a saddened but determined expression. However, John's masking attempt would not be very convincing; he is quite literally keeping a "stiff upper lip."

Figure 58 shows two examples of sadness (brows/forehead and eyes/upper eyelids) and disgust (mouth and lower eyelids). Viewing a battlefield, John might feel sad about the loss of life and disgusted with mankind for such slaughter.

Figure 59 shows blends of sadness (brows/forehead) with happiness

Figure 58

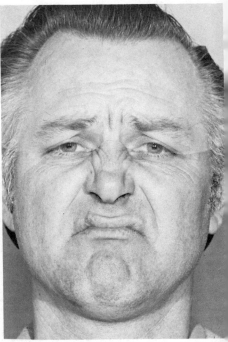

Figure 59

(mouth); in Patricia's expression the eyelids are sad, in John's the upper eyelids are sad while the lower eyelids are happy. These expressions could occur with nostalgic, bittersweet experiences, or when the happy expression is being used as a mask—"laughing on the outside, crying on the inside, because I'm still in love with you." Or when someone says "cheer up, it's not so bad; let's see a smile."

Review

Figure 60 shows two full sadness expressions. Note each of the distinctive clues to sadness.

—The inner corners of the eyebrows are drawn up.

—The skin below the eyebrow is triangulated, with the inner corner up.

—The upper eyelid inner corner is raised.

—The corners of the lips are down or the lip is trembling.

making faces

1. Take facial piece C and place it over the faces in Figure 60. What does does it look like? It should look slightly sad, because you have made

126

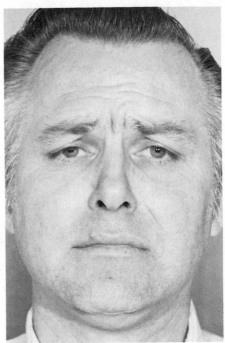

Figure 60

the expression in which sadness is shown only in the brow, as in Figure 51. Note that there is one difference; you are not able to get the sadness upper eyelid to cover the top of the neutral eye as it would appear in sadness (shown in Figure 51). Nevertheless, it still looks sad.

2. Take piece B and put it over the pictures in Figure 60. Now Patricia shows what might be a pout (see Figure 53), but it is a little ambiguous. And John's look is also ambiguous, maybe with the slightest trace of beginning sadness.

3. Take piece D and put it over the pictures in Figure 60. They both look pretty sad, but not as sad as when the mouth is involved. Remove piece D and quickly put it back, so you can see the change.

4. To see a gradation of intensity in sadness, in rapid succession put piece B over the pictures in Figure 60 (slightest sadness), remove B and put piece D over the pictures in Figure 60 (more sadness), and then uncover the pictures in Figure 60 (more sadness).

flashing faces

Check the instructions for Flashing Faces on pages 63-64. Now you can add happy and sad faces, and blends of happiness and sadness with anger, disgust, fear and surprise. First practice the happy, sad faces and blends of these two emotions. When you have them perfect, add the anger, disgust, fear and surprise pictures you practiced with earlier (pages 64 and 98). Practice until you are able to get them all correct.

List of Faces for Flashing Faces, Practice Three:

Figure Number:	*Answers:*
43A	Slight Happy
43B	Moderate Happy
43C	Moderate to Extreme Happy
44A	Moderate Happy
44B	Moderate Happy
45A	Slight Happy
46A	Happy-Surprise Blend
47C	Happy-Contempt Blend
48, left photo	Happy-Anger Blend
48, right photo	Happy-Anger Blend
52A	Slight to Moderate Sadness
54A	Full Face Sadness
54B	Full Face Sadness
55, left photo	Sad-Fear Blend
55, right photo	Sad-Fear Blend
58, left photo	Sad-Disgust Blend
58, right photo	Sad-Disgust Blend
59, left photo	Happy-Sad Blend
59, right photo	Happy-Sad Blend

10

practice faces

Now that you have studied the blueprints of facial expression for each of the six emotions, you are ready to practice what you have learned. Up until now everything has been shown with photographs of just two people, Patricia and John. But now, looking at the pictures of new people, you will see how the blueprints of facial expression vary in minor ways when shown by different people. If what you have learned in each chapter is to become a skill, operative without your needing to think through each step in judging emotion, then you must practice with these new, varied faces.

Cut out the pictures on pages 175-202 at the back. You might want to mount each picture on index cards, with paste or sticky-tape, so the pictures don't become frayed. If you do so, be certain to transfer the number on the back of each picture to the back of the index cards. You will use these numbers to look up the answers at the end of this chapter.

When you have all the pictures cut out, shuffle them and place the deck face up in front of you. Cut out page 204, which you will use to record your judgments of these pictures. Here are the steps to follow:

1. Take a picture off the top of the deck, holding it so you can't see it. (You might put the deck over to the side, so you can't easily see the faces, and without turning your head, reach over to pick up the pictures one at a time.)
2. Close your eyes and hold the picture at a comfortable distance from your face.
3. Blink your eyes open and closed quickly. Once!
4. Judge the emotion.
5. Open your eyes, write down the picture number in the first column of your answer sheet, and your blink-judgment in the second column.
6. Look at the picture for a few seconds, and if your opinion changes write down your second judgment in the third column.

7. Do *not* check the correct answer on the back yet. Instead, place the picture face up in a second pile, go to the next picture, and repeat steps 1 to 6.

8. After judging all the pictures, take the deck and check each of your answers against the information at the end of this chapter.

9. If your blink-judgment was correct, congratulate yourself and go on to the next picture.

10. If your blink-judgment was wrong but your second judgment was correct, take a look at the picture and flash it a few times, blinking your eyes. Try to see what it is that you are missing about it. Put the picture aside, and after you have gone through the deck, check to see if you were failing to be correct in the blink-judgment of pictures of a particular emotion, or if your errors were spread across the emotions. If it was mostly one or two emotions, go back and reread those chapters. If you missed pictures from across the emotions, follow step 12.

11. If your blink-judgment was wrong and your second judgment was also wrong, put the picture aside and go on to the next picture. Each time you have a wrongly judged picture, put it on this same spot, building up a pile. Once you have checked all the pictures, determine from this pile if you were tending to miss mostly pictures of one or two emotions. If so, study the pictures, and go back and restudy the chapters that those pictures are based on. Compare each picture you missed with the figures it refers to. If your errors were distributed pretty evenly across emotions, then just check the wrong pictures against the figures referred to, trying to determine why you made erroneous judgments.

12. After having checked all your judgments, shuffle the deck and go through it again.

Don't expect to be correct on most of the pictures the first time through. You will probably miss more than half. Don't be discouraged. It does take practice! You will probably have to go through the deck anywhere from three to ten times, studying after each time through. Don't go through the deck more than two or three times in a sitting. It is good to let some time elapse so that you will forget the particular pictures.

If you have read this far without deciding whether you want to go through all of this work, read on to the next chapter. You will learn about facial deceit, but you will find that you can't use the information from that chapter unless you have gone through the practice in this chapter. You can then decide. It may be enough to know about it without being able to use it.

Answers

1. Surprise, as shown in Figure 11.
2. Surprise, as in Figure 11. Note that the horizontal wrinkles are quite

subtle in this expression as compared to pictures 1 or 3. Also note that the mouth is only slightly open, as in Figure 9A.

3. Surprise, as in Figure 9A.

4. Surprise, as in Figure 11. If you called it Fear or Fear-Surprise Blend, that is not a bad error. The mouth in this picture is just on the edge of showing a fear element. Compare the mouth with Figure 16. Is it like the face on the left or the right? It is in between. The eyes/lids in this picture are very good examples of surprise. The brow/forehead also shows surprise well. Compare Picture 4 with Picture 11, and note the differences across the face between this person's fear and surprise expressions. Also compare Picture 4 with Figure 20F, a fear-surprise blend, to confirm that Picture 4 is showing surprise, not a blend of fear and surprise.

5. Surprise, as in Figure 11. The mouth is only slightly parted as in Figure 9A. There is no sclera showing above or below the iris, but the surprise blueprint is shown in the brow/forehead and lower face.

6. Surprise, as in Figure 11. No sclera shows above or below the iris in this face, because the eyes are deeply set. The surprise blueprint is shown well in the brow/forehead and in the lower face.

7. Surprise, as in Figure 9. If you called this picture Fear, it was probably because this person's eyebrows are less arched. They are more straightened than is usual in the surprise expression. Note that it is a surprise brow/forehead: There is no drawing together of the eyebrows; there are no vertical wrinkles between the eyebrows; and the horizontal wrinkles are not short, but run across the entire brow.

8. Questioning Surprise, as in Figure 10A. Surprise is shown in the brows/forehead and eyes/lids, with no involvement of the lower face. Compare with Picture 3.

9. Fear, as in Figure 22A. Compare this picture to Picture 2. The brows are drawn together and raised in Picture 9, but the drawing together is slight. The mouth in Picture 9 is similar to that in Figure 18B.

10. Fear, as in Figure 22. Fear is registered very slightly in the lower face in this picture; it is most like that shown in Figure 18A. Compare it with Figure 9A and note the slight hint of a stretching mouth in this picture, which shows it is a slight version of fear rather than a slight surprise mouth.

11. Fear, as in Figure 22B. Compare with Picture 4.

12. Fear, as in Figure 18C.

13. Fear, showing elements of Figure 18A (lower face) and Figure 22A (brow/forehead). The brow/forehead is drawn together but not raised, as it should be in fear.

14. Slight Fear, as in Figure 18A. The lower face shows just the beginning trace of stretching of the lips. The brow/forehead shows a slight sign of raising of the brow but no sign of drawing together. The strongest fear element is the tension in the eyes/lids.

15. Disgust-Contempt—both answers are correct. This picture shows nose-wrinkling and narrowing of eyes as is evident in Figure 24B and lips as in Figure 25C.

16. Disgust, as in Figure 23B.

17. Disgust, as in Figure 24A. If you called this Disgust-Anger Blend, that could be considered a correct answer also, because the brows/forehead are a bit ambiguous. The wrinkling between the brows and this amount of lowering could suggest the presence of anger. The disgust is strongly registered in the lower face and lower eyelids.

18. Disgust, as in Figure 24A.

19. Disgust-Contempt, as in Figure 25C. Both answers are correct.

20. Contempt, as in Figure 25A. Compare with Pictures 32 and 49.

21. Disgust, as in Figure 24B. If you called this Anger, it is probably because of the static signal system. This person has eyebrows set low in his forehead. Check his neutral expression, shown in Picture 52.

22. Contempt, as in Figure 25A. If you called it Anger or Anger-Contempt Blend, check the answer for Picture 21.

23. Slight Anger, as in Figure 36B. The clues to anger are subtle and most easily seen by comparing this anger expression with this person's neutral expression, as shown in Picture 53. In anger the brow is slightly lower and slightly drawn together. The lips are slightly tensed. The most obvious signal is in the staring eyes and tensed lower eyelids.

24. Anger, as in Figure 42B. The anger mouth may involve any one of a number of variations on a square shape. Compare this mouth with the mouth in Pictures 25 and 27 and Figure 34.

25. Anger, as in Figure 42B. See the commentary on Picture 24.

26. Anger, as in Figure 42A.

27. Anger, combining elements of Figure 36B (brow/forehead) and 42B (eyes and lower face). The brows are down, but not drawn close together; the mouth shows the clenched-teeth variation on the open-mouth anger. See the commentary on Picture 24.

28. Anger. This particular combination of elements was not shown in a figure. The brows/forehead, upper eyelid, and staring appearance to the eye are similar to the photographs in Figure 37. The lower eyelid is not tensed and raised. The mouth position is somewhat like Figure 34A and 34B, but less intense. It is more like the mouth position shown in Figure 57A.

29. Anger, as in Figure 36B. If you missed it, you probably called it Fear, failing to distinguish the piercing look of anger from that of fear; compare with Picture 9. In Picture 29 the brows are down (but not drawn together); the lower eyelid is tensed, and the upper lip is pressed slightly down against the lower lip.

30. Happiness, as in Figure 50B.

31. Happiness, as in Figure 50B.
32. Slight Happiness, as in Figure 45A. If you called this Contempt, compare Picture 32 with Pictures 20 and 49.
33. Happiness, as in Figure 50A.
34. Happiness, as in Figure 50B. If you called it Surprise or Happiness-Surprise Blend, it was probably because of the shape of the lips in this picture. To see that it does not involve surprise in the lower face, compare this picture with Figure 46.
35. Happiness, as in Figures 43B and 44B.
36. Happiness, as in Figure 50B.
37. Sadness, as in Figure 54A. Note the gaze down, the corners of the lips down, the slight raising and drawing together of the inner corners of the eyebrows.
38. Sadness, as in Figure 54. A good example of the drawing together and raising of the inner corners of the eyebrows.
39. Slight Sadness, as in Figures 51A and 52A. Don't be concerned, if you were wrong on this picture. Congratulate yourself if you were right. The clues are very subtle. There is the slight trace of the sadness brow, giving a slight triangulation to the upper eyelid. The lower lip may be also beginning to show a trace of sadness, but it is not certain.
40. Sadness, as in Figure 52. Note the drawn-together and slightly raised inner corners of the eyebrow, and the resultant triangulation of the upper eyelid. The gaze is also down. Although the corners of the lips appear down, checking this person's neutral expression (Picture 54) shows that this is the shape of this person's lips.
41. Sadness, but more subtly shown than in any of the figures. How do you know that this person looks sad? Where is the clue? Cover the eyes and forehead with your hand; does the mouth area look sad? No. Cover the lower face with your hand, and you will see that the clue to sadness is in the eyes/lids and brow/forehead. There has been a slight raising of the cheeks, producing a very slight raising of the lower eyelid. The inner corners of the eyebrows have been slightly raised and drawn up, but that is not apparent from the appearance of the eyebrows on this person; it is apparent in the shape of the skin below the eyebrow. Note how it has been triangulated, just as in Figure 51A.
42. Sadness, as in Figure 54B. The mouth shows a very slight hint of sadness.
43. Sadness, as in Figure 54. Even though the lips are slightly parted, sadness is still registered in the downed corners.
44. Sadness, as in Figure 52. This picture shows that on some people the drawing-together and raising muscular action doesn't change the brows; but you can see the pull of the muscles themselves in bunching under the skin in the forehead. Also note the triangulation of the skin under the brow. Also note the wrinkle pattern in the forehead, which occurs

with some people, when the sadness brow is shown. This wrinkle pattern looks like the Greek letter Omega, and has been called the Omega pattern.

45. Happiness-Surprise Blend, as in Figure 46A.

46. Happiness-Surprise Blend, as in Figure 46A.

47. Fear-Surprise Blend, as in Figure 20E. Compare this picture with the fear expression of this person shown in Picture 14. The surprise element in the blend in Picture 47 is the brow/forehead. Picture 47 has the fear mouth shown in Figure 15A, while Picture 14 has the fear mouth shown in Figure 15B.

48. Fear-Surprise Blend, as in Figure 20F. The fear element is in the lower face (Figure 15A), with surprise in the brows/forehead and eyes/lids. The fact that the eyes are opened very wide, which could happen in surprise, also melds easily into a fearful expression.

49. Happiness-Contempt Blend, as in Figure 47C. Compare this picture with this same person's slight happiness expression (Picture 32), and contempt expression (Picture 20). The mouth position is the same in contempt and happiness-contempt. The happiness is registered in this blend expression by the lifting of the cheek and the consequent slight narrowing of the eye.

50. Anger-Disgust Blend, as in Figure 39A. Compare this with Picture 23, in which this person shows anger without disgust (compare the lower face in the two pictures).

51. Sadness-Fear Blend. This type of blend was not shown earlier. It is composed of sadness, registered in the brow/forehead and eyes/lids (Figure 60), and fear in the lower face (Figure 15A). The slight raise in the upper lip may give some hint of contempt. Figure 55 showed another type of fear-sadness blend, in which the fear was registered in the lower face with the more spread fear mouth (Figure 15B).

52. Neutral

53. Neutral

54. Neutral

11

facial deceit

People regard facial expressions of emotion as more trustworthy than words. Everyone has had the experience of being able, or thinking he was able, to tell that what someone said was a lie from the look on his face. No matter what your political persuasion, there was probably at least one witness in the Senate Watergate Hearings whose facial expressions proved to *you* that he was lying. Yet nearly everyone has been taken in by facial expressions of emotion. You might have been misled by a lie of commission, when the person's face showed some feeling which later you learned he in no way felt. Or it might have been a lie of omission, when the person showed no trace on his face of how he actually did feel. And it is not just the actor or politician who can so convincingly lie with his face. Nearly everyone tries, some of the time.

People learn to control and disguise their facial expressions. Children are not only taught what they should not say, but what looks they should not allow on their face. "Don't you look angry at me!" "Wipe that look off your face!" It is not only inhibition that is required, but putting on false faces, usually smiling ones. "Smile at that nice man; he wants to help you." Well before adulthood most people have learned how to manage their facial expressions to meet the demands of society, how to control the messages they give with their face as well as their words.

Facial expressions of emotion are not easy to control. Most people manage their facial expressions, but far from perfectly. People are more *practiced* in lying with words than with faces (and more practiced with faces than with body movement). This is probably because people are held more accountable for their words than for their facial expression. There is more comment on what you say than on what you show in your face. (But there is more comment on what is shown in facial expression than in body movement). Because you are held more responsible for your words than your facial expressions, you become a better performer. But the difference between words and faces in this regard is not great.

It is easier to *monitor* your words as you speak them than to monitor your facial expressions. There are two reasons. First, facial expressions can be extremely rapid, flashing on and off the face in less than a second. With words you can easily take the stance of the person who receives your message, listening to it as he does; this is not as easy with facial expressions. You can hear yourself speak, managing what you are saying word by word, and even changing within a word. But you can't see your own facial expressions, and to do so would be disruptive. Instead you must rely upon a less accurate source of information about what is going on in your face—the feedback from the facial muscles.

It is easier to *falsify* words than facial expressions. You have been explicitly taught to speak; you have learned the vocabulary and grammar. There is not only a dictionary for reference, but also a thesaurus. You can write down exactly what you will say ahead of time. You can rehearse it aloud. A friend can listen to your performance and provide useful criticism by pointing to the word or clause that is off. Try that with your facial expressions. Your critic won't have many terms with which to tell you what is wrong in your face; his opinions are based on only hunches or intuitions. And such vague criticism doesn't help you change your expressions. You don't have anything like a dictionary of facial expressions. You were never taught how to speak with your face. What you learned about facial expression was not which muscles to move for each emotion, but the need to control your facial appearance.

It is much easier to *inhibit* what you reveal in your words than what you reveal in your face. One reason has already been mentioned—the speed of facial expression. But there is a more important reason. The facial expressions that are triggered during the experience of an emotion are involuntary (although they can be interfered with), and the words are not. Suppose you are walking down the street and a ferocious, rabid-looking dog comes racing at you, in full bark. In fear, your heart begins to beat faster, your breathing quickens, other changes occur in your body, and your facial muscles are triggered, so that one of the blueprints shown in Chapter 5 appears. These changes in your face and body occur automatically, without much we could call thought or consideration. There is no similar automatic, involuntary set of words that would burst out of your mouth at that instant, though you might gasp or scream. Words are not impelled by the same type of internal mechanisms that trigger the beat of your heart, the rate of your breathing, or the movement of your facial muscles. To say that these responses are involuntary is not to imply that they can't be controlled. You can breathe rapidly any time you want to, just as you can put on a face when you want to. However, the capacity to falsify doesn't mean that there are not occasions when you will breathe more quickly, not out of choice but because you are gripped by an emotion. When afraid, you could get your breathing *under control,* but this means that you would be contending with and overcoming contrary impulses. It would be a struggle. The same is true with facial expressions.

Because people are less practiced in controlling facial expressions, less able to monitor, falsify, or inhibit their faces than their words, facial expression offers the promise of revealing how someone really feels. But because people are taught to control their facial appearance, because they can override an involuntary facial response or put on a face they don't at all feel, the expression can fool you. In a conversation, facial expressions may be more truthful than words. (There are, of course, clues to deceit in words. Slips of the tongue are obvious examples.) But faces may be even more misleading than words.

Which is which? How do you tell genuine expressions of emotion from phony ones? How can you detect the leakage of feelings the person is trying to conceal from you? Most people follow fairly simple rules:

—The eyes are the most truthful.

—If he says in words he feels an emotion but doesn't show any emotion, you distrust the words. For example, he says he's angry and looks neutral, or says he's happy and looks neutral.

—If he says in words he feels a negative emotion and shows a smile on his face, maybe you trust the words, or maybe you trust the smile. It depends upon the situation. For example, if he says he is afraid of the dentist and smiles, you interpret the smile not as a negation but as a social comment and trust the words. But if a woman disappoints a man (or vice versa) in an appealing way, and he says he is angry but shows a smile, then one distrusts the words.

—If he doesn't say it in words but shows it facially, you believe what the face says, particularly if he denies it in words. For example, if he says "I'm not at all surprised," but looks surprised, then you believe he is surprised.

These rules probably work part of the time, but they can be improved upon. In order to explain more about trustworthy and untrustworthy facial expressions, we first need to discuss the reasons why people control their facial expressions and the techniques employed to manage the appearance of the face.

Four Reasons Why People Control Facial Expressions

We have coined the phrase *display rules* to describe what people learn, probably quite early in their lives, about the need to manage the appearance of particular emotions in particular situations. For example, middle-class, urban, white, adult males in the United States follow the display rule of not showing fear in public. Their female counterparts in the pre-matron or pre-maternal role follow the display rule of not showing anger in public. Originally, you may learn the display rule by being told what to do and not to do, or you may learn it by observation and imitation without ever being specifically instructed. Once learned, display rules operate as habits, much like driving a car. You don't think about what you are doing unless you find you have made a mistake. People pause to consider what display rule to follow only if they are in strange circumstances (display rules vary from culture to culture) or if they can't figure out what the situation is, what their role is, what is expected of them.

The example we gave of a display rule specified that a particular emotion (fear for males, anger for females) must not be shown in public. Sometimes display rules are more specific in prohibiting a particular facial expression only in a particular role or social situation. For example, at middle-class American weddings, the bride may publicly cry or look sad, as may her parents, but not the groom or his parents. Although display rules generally discourage men from crying, sadness is allowable, but not for the groom at his wedding. Often the display rule will specify not only the forbidden emotion but also the emotion that must be shown in its place. At beauty contests it may seem paradoxical that it is the winners, not the losers, who burst into tears with the emcee's announcement, but this is because of the display rule for winners and losers. Losers in such contests must conceal distress and show at least slight happiness. Winners only have to worry about not looking smug. In the moment before the emcee's announcement all the contestants, fearing disappointment, are concentrating on not crying, but smiling. When the winner is announced, it is she who no longer needs to worry about suppressing tears, and out they come.

Display rules need not absolutely forbid or demand showing a particular emotion, but may instead specify adjustments in the intensity of an emotion. For example, at funerals the mourners should adjust their own expressions of grief in relation to the grief of others. There seems to be a pecking order of legitimate claims to grief. Suppose a middle-aged man has died suddenly. At the funeral, if his secretary were to show more grief on her face than his wife, she would be suggesting something improper about the nature of her relationship to the deceased. Instead, her sad facial expression must be more moderate than that shown by people who have a more legitimate public claim to mourn.

We have been discussing the *cultural* display rules—conventions about facial expression that are followed by all (nonrebellious) members of a given social class, subculture, or culture. Their role in social life is the first, most widely shared reason why people control their facial expressions. The second reason is the role of *personal* display rules—habits that are the product of idio-syncracies in family life. For example, a person may have been brought up never to look angrily at someone in authority, or never to look angrily at someone of the opposite sex. A personal display rule may also be quite general; histrionic persons customarily overintensify all emotional expression; poker-faced persons attempt to maintain a constant neutral facial expression.

People control their facial expressions of emotion, then, because of deeply ingrained conventions (cultural display rules) or idiosyncracies in upbringing (personal display rules). A third reason for facial control is vocational requirement. Actors, obviously, must be skilled in managing their facial expressions. So must good diplomats, trial attorneys, salesmen, politicians, doctors, nurses, and perhaps even teachers. The extent to which people enter such professions partly because they are already talented in controlling their expressions, and the extent to which such expertness develops in the course of their formal training or experience, is not known.

The fourth reason why people control their facial expressions is need of the moment. A guilty prisoner testifying to his innocence is not following a cultural or personal display rule, nor a vocational requirement, unless he is a professional criminal. He lies, with his face as well as his words, to save himself. The embezzler must falsely show surprise when the theft is discovered. The husband must inhibit the smile of pleasure on encountering his lover, if in the presence of his wife.

Usually when a person is said to lie with his face or words, he lies to meet some need of the moment. But all four reasons for controlling facial expression can involve false messages or the omission of messages. It is just that society condemns lying more if it is done for personal gain rather than because of personality, vocational requirement, or its own conventions. The word *lying,* however, may be itself misleading about what occurs. It suggests that the only important message is the true feeling that underlies the false message. But the false message is important as well, if you know it is false. Rather than calling the process lying, we might better call it message control, because the lie itself may convey a useful message.

There are times when people do not engage in controlling the messages they provide; there is no duplicity of messages; the information provided is internally consistent. This is frank or honest communication. There are times when people engage in message control, trying to conceal one message and substitute another. The messages are then in conflict, one reflecting actual feeling, the other reflecting what the person wants to convey or thinks he should convey. Both messages have information; both are important. Suppose a person has been acutely depressed and, while still depressed, now tries to conceal the sad expression and look moderately happy. You are misled if you think he is happy, not realizing that he is still sad. But you are also misled if you disregard his attempt to look happy, for it might be telling you that he is beginning to feel better, or he is not to be trusted, or he wants to please you, or you don't need to worry so much about him. The question is how to recognize that message control is occurring, and if it is occurring, how to recognize both the message that is felt and the message that is not felt. To answer that question we must first distinguish among the various techniques for facial management. For when people control the messages given by their faces, they do much more than just substitute an unfelt for a felt emotion.

Facial Management Techniques

In managing your facial appearance you can seek to *qualify* the appearance of the emotion you actually feel, or to *modulate* the expression of that feeling, or to *falsify* the message.

qualifying

In qualifying a facial expression, you add a further expression as a comment on the expression you have just shown. For example, if you show fear when the dentist approaches, you may add an element of disgust to your facial expression, as a comment to the dentist that you are disgusted with yourself for being afraid. The felt emotional expression is not changed in its intensity, as in modulating, nor is it concealed or replaced with an unfelt emotional expression, as in falsifying. An emotional expression can be a qualifer when shown immediately after the first one, either as a social comment called for by a cultural or personal display rule or as a genuine expression of a further feeling. The person may actually feel disgusted with himself for being afraid of the dentist or he may be following a display rule to make it clear that he is not completely childish.

The smile is the most frequent qualifier, added as a comment to any of the negative emotions. The smile qualifier gives a clue as to the likely consequences, or limits, of the negative emotion. It tells the other person how seriously to take it. It informs the other person you are still in control. For example, if you smile to qualify an angry expression, you are facially saying you won't go too far; your attack will be limited or suppressed. If the smile is blended with the anger, rather than qualifying it as an after-comment, you are saying that you are enjoying being angry. The smile qualifier to sadness means "I can stand it," "I won't cry again," "I'm not going to kill myself," etc. The smile qualifier to fear means "I'll go through with it anyway," "I'm not going to run away," etc.

Qualifying a facial expression is the mildest form of facial management. It distorts very little, and is usually the result of personal or cultural display rules, not individual needs of the moment. Because the distortion of the message is minimal and the evidence of qualifying is usually obvious, we will not discuss any ways to recognize that an expression has been qualified.

modulating

In modulating a facial expression, you adjust the intensity of the expression to show either more or less than you actually feel. You are not commenting on the emotion message (qualifying) or changing the nature of the message (falsifying), but only increasing or diminishing its intensity. There are three ways to modulate a facial expression. You can vary the number of facial areas involved, the duration of the expression, or the excursion of the facial muscles.

Suppose John, when feeling afraid, was following the display rule to deintensify fear to apprehension. With fear, the full expression involving all three facial areas, shown in Figure 22A, would occur. If he were to deintensify his expression of this feeling, he would do one or more of the following:

—Eliminate fear from the mouth area (as in Figure 19A), and perhaps from the eyes as well (Figure 13B); or show fear only with the mouth (the photograph on the right in Figure 17).
—Shorten the duration of the expression.
—Stretch the mouth less; tense the lower lid less; and not lift and draw together the brow as much.

If John had actually felt only apprehensive but was trying to look afraid, then he would actually have the expression shown in Figure 13B, and reverse the steps outlined for deintensifying in order to intensify the expression. Typically when people modulate, intensifying or deintensifying, they will use all three techniques—changing the number of facial areas involved, how long the expression is held, and how strongly the muscles pull. Later, we will discuss how to recognize a facial expression that has been modulated.

falsifying

In falsifying a facial expression of emotion, you show a feeling when you have none (*simulate*); or you show nothing when indeed you do feel a particular way (*neutralize*); or you cover a felt emotion with the appearance of an emotion you do not feel (*mask*). In simulating you try to give the impression that you are actually experiencing a particular emotion when in fact you are not feeling any emotion. Suppose someone tells you about the misfortune of a presumed close friend and you don't care at all; you have no feeling, but you put on a sad expression. That is simulating.

In order to simulate successfully, you must be able to remember the sensations of what each emotional expression feels like on your face, from the inside, so you can voluntarily adjust your face to look that way to others. Usually you can't anticipate the need to simulate, and don't have the chance to practice in front of a mirror where you can see how you are doing, to rehearse your performance. Children and adolescents often practice facial expressions this way to become skilled, and adults will practice for special occasions for which they have notice. Most often, however, you must rely upon your proprioceptive sensations—what it feels like on the inside of your face. You must be sensitive to those feelings and match them to your memory of how your face felt when you were angry, afraid, etc., so you can voluntarily adjust your face to look a particular way.

Neutralizing is just the opposite of simulating. You have a strong emotion, but you attempt to appear as if you feel nothing. Neutralizing is the extreme of deintensifying; the expression is modulated down to nothing. If John were afraid and his goal was to appear cool and unemotional, then he would be neutralizing. In neutralizing, you try to

—keep the facial muscles relaxed, inhibiting any muscular contraction;
—freeze the facial muscles into a nonemotional poker face; setting the jaw; tightening, but not pressing, the lips; staring, but not tensing the eyelids, etc.;
—camouflage the face by biting the lips, sucking the lips, wiping the eyes, rubbing part of the face, etc.

Neutralizing is very difficult, particularly if there is some strong event or series of events provoking an emotional reaction. Typically, in neutralizing, you will look so wooden or tense that you at least give away the fact that you are falsifying, even if the actual emotion experienced is not revealed. Most often, rather than neutralize, people will mask, which is easier and more successful.

In *masking,* you simulate an emotion that is not felt, to cover or conceal another emotion that is felt. When you heard about the unfortunate incident to your presumed friend and simulated a sad look, it was a simulation only if you felt nothing. If you had felt disgust and covered it with the sad look, that would be masking. People mask because it is easier to conceal one facial expression with another than it is to try to show nothing. And people mask because their reason for hiding a particular emotion usually requires the false statement of a replacement. For example, if a depressed person is not to be suspected of still thinking of suicide, he must not only neutralize sadness but also show happiness. The smile, which we earlier noted was the most common emotion qualifier, is also the most common emotion mask. Darwin first suggested a reason for this. The muscular movements required for smiling are

most different from the muscular movements involved in the negative emotions. Strictly on an anatomical basis, the smile best conceals the appearance
in the lower face of anger, disgust, sadness, or fear. And, of course, often the
very nature of the social situation that might motivate you to conceal one of
those emotions would lead you to want to substitute the friendly message of
the smile. There are also occasions when people mask a negative emotion with
another negative emotion—anger over fear, for example, or sadness over
anger. And sometimes people mask a happy expression with a negative one.

All three management techniques—qualifying, modulating, and falsifying (which includes simulating, neutralizing, and masking)—may occur for
any of the four reasons people control their facial expression—cultural display
rules, personal display rules, vocational requirement, or need of the moment.

Obstacles to Recognizing Facial Management

How can you tell if someone is managing his facial expressions, particularly if he is falsifying, in which case the information would be most misleading? Most of the time you can probably tell with no difficulty, because most
facial management is the product of cultural display rules, and is not performed
very well. You probably are aware when someone is following a cultural
display rule, but the same set of factors that led someone to manage his facial
expression will cause you to ignore any errors or "gaffes" he makes. You may
even want to be misled, or at least not to acknowledge that you actually know
how the person truly feels. Think of all the times you have said, "How are
you today?"—not really wanting to know, ignoring everything in the person's
facial expression other than the perfunctory smile which the cultural display
rule always calls for on initial greeting.

Often it's not that you need to be taught how to recognize facial management, but instead that a large part of the time you unwittingly ignore errors
others make in their facial expressions. You have been trained to cooperate, at
least sometmes, in maintaining falsification in the emotional information you
get from others. Although this is most usual when people are following cultural
display rules, because social forces affect both the person who shows the
expression and the person who sees it, you may engage in such collusion even
when a person is purposefully trying to deceive you, to fill his own need of
the moment. A wife can ignore the rough edges in the facial lies of her philan-
dering husband because she doesn't want to have to confront the situation; and
she may or may not be aware of her participation in the secret.

Sometimes you recognize that facial management is occurring because
the other person wants you to recognize it, but neither of you acknowledges it.
This is almost always the case when a facial expression is *qualified,* when a

comment is added. The smile qualifier is added to an otherwise fearful face so that the other person will see the qualifier, realize that the fear will be endured without flight, or screams, etc. Sometimes a facial expression is *modulated* in such a way as to make it obvious that the expression has been intensified or diminished. Suppose you want the person who has provoked you to know that you are furious but are controlling yourself and won't physically attack in return. One way to convey that message is to show a deintensified-anger facial expression, where the deintensifying is obvious. The other person knows you are furious, but he also knows you are managing it. Similarly, sometimes facial expressions are *falsified* in such a way that the message is obviously false. The falsifier can want everyone to know his expression is false. A person who is genuinely mourning may for a moment mask his real feeling of grief with a smile when first greeting an old friend who has come to pay his respects. The smile may be half-hearted, a token to the greeting ritual, with no attempt to conceal the actually felt distress or sadness.

But what of those situations in which facial expression is modulated or falsified in a way intended to fool you, to mislead you about how the person actually feels? Where you really do want to know how the other person actually is feeling, not just what he wants you to think he feels. With some people you probably will have little chance to spot when they are controlling their facial expression. They are just too good for you to detect signs of facial management. A really good actor is very convincing, and so is a really good salesman, or trial attorney. All you can really know, if you are up against such an expert, is that you had better not take his facial expression at face value, because he's a pro. Unfortunately, there are professional facial liars who are not salesmen or actors or trial attorneys; they are just good at fooling people with their facial expressions. They usually know it, and their friends come to know it. In our current research, we are trying to understand just what characterizes people who, without special training, become such professional facial deceivers. But we don't have much to report yet. Fortunately, most people are not that good.

If you do not want to be misled, and if you are not dealing with a professional facial liar, then you need to recognize signs of *leakage* and *deception clues*. Leakage can be defined as the nonintended betrayal of a feeling the person is trying to conceal. A deception clue tells you that facial management is occurring, but not what the concealed emotion is; you simply know that something is amiss. When a person is attempting to neutralize the anger he actually feels, if he does a poor job, you may still see a trace of his anger (leakage). Or he may successfully neutralize it with a poker face, but his face looks sufficiently awkward for you to know he is not showing how he really feels (deception clue). Suppose he masks the felt anger with a sad expression. The anger may still leak through. Or it may not, but the sad look may be unconvincing—a deception clue that some other emotion is being concealed. Suppose the anger is modulated, deintensified to minor annoyance; again, there could be leakage of the more intense anger, or just a deception clue that something is amiss with the expression of annoyance.

Sources of Leakage and Deception Clues

We will discuss four aspects of facial expression which may tell you that a person is controlling his facial expressions. The first is facial *morphology,* the particular configuration of the appearance of the face. All the earlier chapters have focused upon morphology, the temporary changes in the shape of the facial features and wrinkles that convey emotion. As we will explain, one part of the face is more often disguised than others, but just where to look for the false and the felt feeling does vary with particular emotions. The second aspect is the *timing* of an expression—how long it takes to appear on the face, how long it remains, and how long it takes to disappear. The third aspect is the *location* of the expression in the conversation. And the fourth is what are called *micro-facial expressions,* which result from interruptions.

All four factors—morphology, timing, location, and micro-expressions—must be interpreted in light of the social context in which an expression occurs. For example, you will learn how to tell from morphology where to look for a trace of fear in what appears to be an angry expression. But to determine whether that trace of fear is leakage of an attempt to conceal fear or a fear-anger blend, you must rely upon the social context. Is it a situation in which a person is likely to experience a fear-anger blend? Is the person acknowledging mixed feelings? Is he denying being afraid? What does his body show, etc.? The social context includes other behaviors (head tilt or movement, body posture, body movement, voice, words); preceding and subsequent behaviors; the behavior of other interactants; the definition of the situation, its social "frame," those social norms which lead you to expect one or another emotion to be experienced. In explaining each of the sources of leakage and deception clues, we will point out when the choice between alternative explanations depends upon the social context, assuming that you will know and attend to the context to make the decision.

morphology

Watch out for what people do in the lower part of the face, particularly the lips and the lines around the nose and lower cheek. Although we do not yet have evidence to prove this, our study of facial expression suggests that when a person is controlling what is shown on his face, more effort is focused on managing what occurs in and around his mouth and lips than in the area of the eyes/lids or brows/forehead. This might be because of the role of the mouth in speech, and the consequent greater awareness a person has of what he does with that part of his face. It might also result from the common practice of inhibiting what emanates from the mouth in the most extreme, uncontrolled emotional expressions—shouting in anger, screaming in terror, moaning and crying in distress, regurgitating or spitting in disgust, laughing in happiness.

When you *modulate* your facial expression, then, intensifying or de-intensifying the appearance of an emotion, you will most likely manage your mouth. If you were very afraid, you could deintensify your fearful expression by eliminating the involvement of the eyelids or brows/forehead; but it is most likely that instead you will eliminate signs of fear in the mouth. Your fear expression could also be deintensified by managing the amount of muscle pull in any of the three facial areas, limiting the muscular contractions. Again, you will most probably focus your management efforts on the mouth, curtailing the muscular contractions here more than in the eyes/lids or brows/forehead.

In *falsifying* facial expressions, again the mouth is more the focus for management than the eyes/lids or brows/forehead. If the falsifying is accomplished by neutralizing a felt expression, it is most likely that the expression will disappear from the mouth. If the falsifying entails simulating an unfelt emotion, it is most likely that the false expression will appear in the mouth area. If the falsifying involves masking a felt emotion with a simulated emotion, again the mouth is the most likely focus of attention.

Many of the movements of the muscles in and around the lips and mouth also change the configuration of the cheeks, the chin, and the lower eyelids. Put your hands over your face with the tips of your fingers touching your lower eyelids and the heel of your hand over your mouth and chin. Gently pressing your hands and fingers against your face, make each of the lower face movements shown in Figures 7, 15, 23, 34, 43, and 53, paying particular attention to the changes in the lower eyelids that you feel in your fingertips. The upper part of your cheeks and the lower eyelids are most changed by the open-mouth anger, by either of the disgust mouths, and by all of the happy mouths, except for the extremely slight one. For these emotions, modulating or falsifying would be manifest not only in the lower face but also in the cheeks and lower eyelids.

Generally people manipulate the brow/forehead to falsify or modulate less often than the lower face. The movements of the muscles that control the brow/forehead also can affect the appearance of the upper eyelids, particularly in anger and sadness. Predicting how leakage and deception clues will appear during modulation or falsification of each of the emotions depends not only upon the differential role of the three facial areas but also on how practiced a person is in making a particular muscular movement.

Earlier we pointed out that certain of the brow/forehead positions are used as punctuators to emphasize a particular word or phrase, like italics or accent marks. If someone uses such a brow/forehead movement as a punctuator, whether it be the fairly common surprise or anger derivative or even the more rarely used sadness derivative, then it is likely he will be better able to lie with that particular movement. At least, he will be practiced in making that movement.

Some of the facial movements that make up an emotional expression also function as *emblems*. Such an emblem, you will remember, is a muscular movement which both the person doing it and the person seeing it know to be not an expression of feeling but a conventional reference to a feeling; it is akin to mentioning an emotion in a word. The raised brow in surprise was described as an emblem for questioning, the dropped jaw as an emblem for being dumbfounded, etc. If a muscular movement that is part of an emotional expression is also an emblem, then it is likely that people will be able to lie with it well and unlikely that there will be leakage in that area. Taking all of these matters into consideration, we can suggest where to look for leakage and deception clues for each of the six emotions we have discussed.

Recognizing leakage and deception clues in *happiness* expressions depends upon the fact that this is the one emotion that has no specific brow/forehead movement. If someone is simulating happiness—making a happy face when he feels no emotion at all—we cannot expect to pick up a deception clue from a failure to involve the brow/forehead, because he doesn't need to do this. But by the same token, if he is using happiness as a mask to cover another emotion, he cannot assume a happy brow/forehead, and there may well be leakage of the actually felt emotion in the upper eyelids and brow/forehead. When happiness expressions are deintensified, there may still be a trace of the expression left in the slight raising of the cheeks, slight dimpling in the corners of the lips, and the slight wrinkling of the lower eyelid, even when the smile has been erased.

Surprise is easily simulated, because both the mouth and brow movements involved are also surprise-related emblems. (Figure 5 showed the questioning emblem of the surprise brow, and Figure 8 showed the dumbfounded emblem of the surprise mouth.) Perhaps the only deception clue in simulated surprise will be the absence of the opened but relaxed eyelids. But this may just as well be a less interested or dazed surprise (Figure 10C). If the social context doesn't suggest less interested or dazed surprise, then this would be a deception clue. Later, we will explain how simulations may be detected through imperfections in their timing, not just mistakes in facial-area involvement. Timing is probably the best source of deception clues about simulated surprise.

Surprise may often be used to mask fear, but probably not successfully. It is a likely mask for fear because of similarities in the experience and in the situations that call forth these two emotions. But because of similarities in the muscular movements, the fear is likely to shine through. Surprise can be used to mask any other emotion. For example, if you are told of someone's misfortune and are supposed to feel sad but really feel glad, you may mask with surprise. In fact, some people habitually react with apparent surprise to any piece of information to avoid showing their immediate emotional response (the "ever-ready expressor" discussed in Chapter 12). The clue that the surprise expression is a mask should be timing. It must be prolonged to succeed in concealing, but as we explained earlier, surprise is a brief emotion. If it is prolonged, it is likely to be false.

When someone is simulating *fear,* he will probably assume a fear mouth and staring eyes, so look for a blank brow/forehead. This may be a deception clue, but it may also be an indication of the more horrified or shocked fear, which doesn't involve the brow (pictures on the right of Figure 19); the choice depends upon the social context. A fear expression with a blank brow/forehead may also occur because this particular person doesn't make that brow movement. This is one instance of an obvious but important general principle. *You have a better chance of detecting facial management if you are familiar with the idiosyncrasies of a person's repertoire of facial expressions,* with what he does with his face when he genuinely feels and expresses each emotion. The fear brow/forehead configuration may never be shown by some people. Although many people show it when they are actually afraid, it is difficult to simulate, because it is not easy to make voluntarily. And the fear brow/forehead position is not an emblem or a punctuator, as are the surprise and anger brows. Therefore, when the fear brow is shown, it is a reliable indicator of fear. Occurring alone in an otherwise neutral face, the fear brow/forehead indicates genuine fear—perhaps slight, or perhaps intense and controlled. If the fear brow occurs with the rest of the face showing another emotion, it indicates a blend, or that the other parts of the face are being masked. The context will tell you which. For example, if a fear brow is joined by a happy mouth and lower eyelid (as shown in Figure 49), it is most likely that the happy part of the expression is a mask, unless there is something in the occasion which suggests that the person could be both happy and afraid. If fear was used to mask some other emotion, the brow/forehead would not be employed, and the actual felt emotion might be evident there.

When *anger* is simulated, there may be no clear deception clue from the involvement of the different facial areas. Although we have said that the brow/forehead is usually not involved in facial management, the lowered, drawn-together brow that is part of anger (see Figure 31) is also an emblem for determination, concentration, or perplexity. This brow/forehead position is very easy to make; it is also a punctuator. Therefore, you can expect the brow/forehead to be recruited as part of simulated anger. Simulating anger in the lower face, particularly the closed-lip-press mouth (Figure 34), can also be quite easily done. The only element missing in an anger simulation may be a lack of tension in the lower eyelid, a subtle deception clue indeed. Deintensifying anger may similarly operate primarily on the brow/forehead and lower face. When anger is used as a mask, it will be shown in both the lower face and the brow/forehead, leaving only the eyelids to leak the actual feeling. When another emotion is used as a mask to cover anger, the felt anger may leak through in the stare of the eyes, the tension of the lower lid, and the drawing together of the brow.

Disgust is easily simulated, because there are three disgust emblems—nose-wrinkling, raising the upper lip, and raising one side of the upper lip (see Figure 25). The brow/forehead plays such a minor role in the disgust facial expression that its absence wouldn't be noticeable. (If the brow/forehead of disgust survived intact when the lower face was diminished by deintensifying, it would not be a very clear sign of the emotion.) When disgust is used as a mask, it is probably most often used to mask anger. The leakage of anger might be spotted in the brow, if the brow is not only drawn down, as in disgust, but also drawn together (as shown in Figure 38C). Or it might be seen in the hard tense-lids stare of anger joined with the disgust lower face (as in Figure 39A). But these expressions could be blends if the situation called forth both disgust and anger. If the person denies anger in a clearly anger-evoking situation or only mentions disgust, then it would be more likely that disgust is a mask over anger. The same thing would happen if disgust is being used to mask fear; fear would probably still be evident in the brow/forehead and the sclera above the iris in the eye (see Figure 29). Whether it is a blend or evidence of masking would depend upon the social context, particularly in what the person says and does. Because the only strong element in the disgust expression is in the lower face, and it is the lower face that is used most readily in simulating, it is likely that attempts to mask disgust with another facial appearance will succeed. At best, there may be a trace of the underlying disgust in a slight raise in the upper lip or a hint of nose-wrinkling when another emotion masks disgust.

When *sadness* is simulated, it will probably be shown in the lower face and a downward cast of the eyes. The absence of the sad brow/forehead and upper eyelid would be a good clue that the sadness was simulated. As with the fear brow/forehead, the sad brow/forehead is a particularly reliable indicator that sadness is genuinely felt, because this expression is hard to make voluntarily; it is not part of a facial emblem, and it is rarely used as a punctuator. Some people, however, never show the sad brow/forehead, even when they are genuinely sad. As we emphasized in discussing fear, *you must know whether or not a particular muscular movement is part of the person's usual repertoire to infer leakage or deception clues reliably.* If the brow/forehead is not part of the person's repertoire when he is actually sad, then its absence won't tell you that an otherwise sad expression is a simulation. With such people you will have to look at the shape of the upper eyelid. It should be pulled up at the inner corners if the person is actually sad, even if he doesn't show the sad brow/forehead; but this is a more subtle cue. If the sad brow/forehead is part of the person's repertoire when he is *not* sad, again, your ability to detect a simulation would be affected. It is the rare person who uses the sad brow/forehead as a punctuator, but such a person may be able to fool you when he simulates sadness by employing his brow/forehead (and upper eyelid) in his performance.

When a person deintensifies the sad expression, the brow/forehead and upper eyelid are most likely to survive as leakage of the actually felt intensity. If the sadness expression is being masked by another emotion, the sad brow/forehead and upper eyelid are most likely to leak through. And when sadness is itself used to mask another emotion—unless it is done by one of those atypical people who punctuate with the sad brow/forehead—the sad mask will fail to cover the felt emotion leaking in the brow/forehead.

timing

You can become aware of facial management, in particular of deception clues, by being sensitive to the *timing* of a facial expression. How long does it take for the expression to appear on the face (onset time)? How long does the expression remain on the face before it starts to recede or change into another expression (duration)? And how long does it take for the expression to disappear (offset time); does it linger, fading gradually, or disappear, or shift abruptly? There is no hard and fast general rule to tell you what the onset, duration, and offset are for each of the emotions. We cannot say that anger must take no longer than 1.3 seconds to appear, cannot remain for more than 7 seconds, and abruptly disappear. That obviously would be fallacious. Timing depends upon the social context, but the requirements of each situation can be quite exacting. Suppose you were simulating enjoyment when someone who tells terrible jokes is telling his latest. How long it takes for the smile to appear on your face (onset time) depends upon the buildup to the punch line (whether it is gradual, with slightly humorous elements, or abrupt) and the nature of the punch line (whether it is delivered abruptly or stretched out). How long the smile stays on your face (duration time) depends on how funny the joke is, whether there is another joke following, etc. How long it takes for the smile to disappear or fade from your face (offset time) depends upon what is said next, your relationship to the joke-teller, etc. In faking enjoyment everyone knows the morphology—to pull the corners of the lips up and back, perhaps opening the mouth slightly, and allowing the corners of the eyelids to wrinkle—but people are not usually as good in adjusting the onset, duration, and offset time. If you watch carefully, you will know when the timing is off, and this can be crucial in spotting deception clues.

location

Closely related to the timing of a facial expression is its *location* in the conversational stream—just where the expression is placed in relationship to the words—and its juxtaposition with body movement. Suppose you were going to simulate anger, telling someone in words that you are fed up with his behavior when in fact you don't feel much one way or another, but you are supposed to act angry. You would want to show the anger in your face, not just in words; otherwise you might not be believed. Where you place that angry facial expression matters. If the angry facial expression comes after the verbal statement ("I'm fed up with you" . . . 1.5 seconds . . . and then the angry expression), it looks false. Showing the expression early, let us say before the "I'm fed up with you" line, won't be a deception clue if it continues into the verbalization. It will suggest that you are thinking, or having difficulty deciding whether to express or how to express your anger.

There is probably less latitude in the juxtaposition of facial expression and body movement. Suppose during the "I'm fed up" line you banged your fist on a table and showed the facial expression before but not during the fist-bang, or afterward. If facial expressions are not synchronized with the concomitant body movement, they look put on.

micro-expressions

In deintensifying, neutralizing, or masking a facial expression, sometimes a person will interrupt an expression as it is occurring rather than intercepting it in advance of any muscular movement. This provides a fourth source of leakage and deception clues, the *micro-expression*. (We have already discussed morphology, timing, and location.)

Although most facial expressions last more than one second, micro-expressions last well under a second—perhaps $\frac{1}{5}$ to $\frac{1}{25}$ of a second. At least some of these micro-expressions are the result of interruptions, where the felt facial expression is interfered with. You feel afraid, the expression begins to appear on your face, you sense from your facial muscles that you are beginning to look afraid, and you deintensify the expression, neutralize it, mask it. For a fraction of a second the fear expression will have been there. Micro-expressions are typically embedded in movement, often in facial movements that are part of talking. And they are typically followed immediately by a masking facial expression. We know from our research that most people don't pay attention to or don't actually see these micro-expressions, but that everyone with good vision *can* see them. It takes some practice to know what to look for. You can practice spotting these very brief expressions by looking at the practice photographs in Chapter 10 while blinking your eyes. This is about the speed of a micro-expression.

Some micro-expressions don't show enough to leak what the emotion was that was being deintensified, neutralized, or masked. They are caught too early. These squelched fragments of a facial expression can still be a clue that the person is managing his facial expression. Some micro-expressions are complete enough to leak the felt emotion. It is possible, although no one has established this for certain, that micro-expressions occur not only when people are purposefully managing their facial expression but also when they are not aware of how they feel, when they are deceiving themselves.

Though micro-expressions are a tantalizing source of information, some cautions must be given. If a person doesn't show a micro-expression, that doesn't mean he is not deintensifying, neutralizing, or masking. Some people, as we have said, are professional facial liars, and others are awfully good at facial deception even though their work doesn't require it. Still others may show leakage and deception clues in the ways we have already discussed (morphology, timing, location) but never show micro-expressions. And people may show a micro-expression in one situation but not in another. Micro-expressions are reliable as deception clues or leakage, but you can't draw any conclusions from their absence.

We should mention that the face is not the only source of leakage and deception clues. Inconsistencies and discrepancies in speech, body movement, and voice are other important clues. We know that people, at least in our culture, tend to manage their facial expressions more than they do their body movements, and perhaps more than their voices. Much of our current research is directed toward isolating the particular body movements that function as leakage and deception clues. If you watch the body, you can detect signs that emotions are being controlled. But to explain just why and describe what to watch is the subject of another whole book, which is still a few years away.

In Chapter 3, when we discussed the research basis for this book, we pointed out that much of what we would be describing about recognizing signs of facial management has not yet been proven. These ideas must be treated as suggestions. Most of them probably are true, but even those do not work for everybody or in every situation. Remember also that there are many things to consider in recognizing facial management.

—Are you really willing to look at a person's face?

—Do you really want to know how the person actually feels, or would you instead prefer to know only what he wants you to know?

—Is the person a professional facial deceiver, by vocation or otherwise?

—Do you know how that person typically looks when he is experiencing the emotion in question and is not controlling his facial expression? (If not, be much more tentative in your judgments.)

—Are you familiar with the facial morphology, the appearance of each emotion in each of the three areas of the face? (Remember, where to look and what to look for varies with each emotion.)

—Do you notice the timing of an expression—its onset, duration, and offset?

—Do you consider the location of the facial expression in the conversational stream?

—Are you alert to micro-expressions?

—Do you compare the facial expressions with the person's body movements, posture, voice tone?

—Are you checking alternative explanations against your knowledge of the social context?

The more ways in which you can detect facial management (morphology, timing, location, micro-expression, contradiction by body movement, or voice tone) and the more frequently you observe it, the more confidence you can have in your assessment of the facial expression of emotion.

12

checking your own facial expression

You have been learning how to read other people's facial expressions. The question now is, what do you do with your own face? Although the main themes—the blueprints of facial expression—are universal, there are individual variations on how those themes are performed. First, the static facial signals make any of the emotional expressions look a bit different, depending upon how high the cheekbones are, how deeply set the eyes, how much fat is deposited below the skin, exactly where the muscles are attached, etc. Second, personal experience leads to differences in what arouses a particular emotion. We have outlined some common events that arouse fear, anger, and so forth, but people are simply not angered by the same events. Third, personal display rules—deeply ingrained habits learned in childhood about managing facial appearance—are different for different persons. Unlike cultural display rules, the personal display rules are individual and not shared by most members of a culture or subculture.

Although all three factors are responsible for many of the variations in facial expression, we will be concerned primarily with characteristic styles of facial expression that result from exaggerations of personal display rules. Personal display rules may be quite specific, referring only to a particular emotion in a particular situation; one, for example, might be not to let anger show in your face when you are angry at your father (or all authority figures). Or personal display rules may be quite exaggerated, quite general in their application; for example, you may have learned never to let anger show in your face, or even never to let *any* emotion show in your face when you are feeling it. These personal display rules can result in a particular cast to someone's facial expression, something characteristically different about his face. We will describe eight characteristic *styles* of facial expression. We will describe these styles in their most extreme form to explain them most clearly. Some people are characterized by one of these extreme styles. Most people show a style only in a less pronounced fashion. You may show one of these styles all the time, only in some situations or roles, only when you are under stress, or only at certain points in your life, etc. After explaining the eight styles, we will outline a rather elaborate series of steps you can take to discover whether or not you are characterized by an extreme version of one of these styles.

Eight Styles of Facial Expression

Are you a *withholder?* Or perchance, are you a *revealer?* These are the first two expressive styles, and they are based simply on whether a person has an expressive or an unexpressive face. Often people think expressiveness depends upon the static facial signals, that it matters whether someone has large eyes, good cheekbones, etc. This is of little consequence. Dark, large eyebrows may make your expression more visible, but the more important factor is the rapid facial signals. In short, do you move your face or not? You must know people whose faces rarely show how they feel. It is not that they are deliberately trying to deceive you, to conceal; they just rarely show their feelings on their faces. And there are their opposites—you always know how these people feel; it is written all over their faces. They are like children in that they can't seem ever to modulate their facial expressions. Sometimes it is embarrassing to you or to them that their feelings always show. They often break the cultural display rules about facial expression; they are just not able to control their expressions.

Revealers usually know about it; they are aware of getting into trouble, at least sometimes, because they show their feelings. They will say they just can't do anything about it. Withholders often know about themselves too, but not invariably.

Do you sometimes not know what is showing on your face? *Unwitting expressors* don't know they are showing how they feel when they are showing it. If you are an unwitting expressor, you may have had the experience of wondering how someone knew you were angry (or afraid, or sad, etc.). If a friend of yours is an unwitting expressor, he may ask you how it is that you know how he felt at a particular moment. He didn't know anything was showing on his face. Unwitting expressors usually specialize; there are only one or two emotions that they show without knowing it.

Does your face actually look blank when you think you are showing anger (or fear, etc.)? *Blanked expressors* are convinced they are showing an emotion on their face when, in fact, their face looks neutral or completely ambiguous to others. Like the unwitting expressor, the blanked expressor specializes. It is a *particular* emotion which he thinks he is showing on his face when he is showing little if anything at all. It is possible that if you are a blanked expressor you may learn about it from others' comments. People may tell you that you don't look the way you sound, that the look on your face doesn't fit what you are saying, etc. Our hunch, however, is that most blanked expressors are not aware of this characteristic.

Do you look disgusted when you actually feel angry and think you look angry? Or do you look sad to others when you feel angry, or angry when you feel sad, etc.? The *substitute expressor* characteristically substitutes the appearance of one emotion for another without knowing what he is doing. Such a person thinks he looks the way he feels, and it is not easy to persuade him that this is not the case. For example, we have shown to substitute expressors videotapes of their faces when they were feeling angry, or trying to look angry, and pointed out that they looked sad. Looking at the videotape of their own faces, their typical reaction has been to deny what we say, insisting that their faces looked angry and not sad, that we were wrong in saying their faces showed sadness. Persuasion has only occurred when we were able to show them that most other people who saw that videotape said they looked sad.

Do you always show a trace of one of the emotions in some part of your face when you are actually not feeling any emotion? Instead of looking neutral, a *frozen-affect expressor's* face may look a bit sad (the corners of the lips are slightly down or the inner corners of the brows are slightly raised) or surprised (the brows are slightly raised) or disgusted/contemptuous (there is a slight raise in the upper lip) or angry (the brows are slightly lowered, or the lips slightly tight) or worried (the brow is slightly raised and drawn together). Such a frozen-affect appearance may result from a trick of nature. The person's face may just be constructed that way. Or it may result from a longstanding habit that maintains a slight muscular contraction on the face when no particular emotion is being experienced. People who are frozen-affect expressors usually do not know it.

Is your initial response to almost anything to look surprised, worried, disgusted, etc.? An *ever-ready expressor* characteristically shows one of the emotions as his first response to almost any event in any situation. His ever-ready expression replaces whatever he might actually feel, which may only be evident afterward. An ever-ready expressor might, for example, show a surprise face to good news, bad news, angry provocations, threats, etc. No matter what happens, surprise is his initial expression. The ever-ready emotion may be any of the ones we have discussed or it may be only part of the facial expression—only the surprise brow, or only the disgust nose-wrinkle, etc. Ever-ready expressors are probably quite unaware of this characteristic style of facial expression.

The last characteristic style of facial expressiveness that we have encountered is the *flooded-affect expressor*. Such a person always shows one or two emotions, in a fairly definite way, almost all the time. There is never a time when he is feeling neutral; the flooded emotion is a continuing part of his feeling state. If any other emotion is aroused, the flooded emotion colors it. For example, if a person is flooded with fear, then he looks at least somewhat afraid all the time; if he becomes angry, he will look angry and afraid or, even more likely, the fear will overwhelm the anger, at least in his appearance. We have seen flooded-affect expressors only among severely disturbed people or people in the midst of a major life crisis. These people and the people around them are keenly aware that they are flooded-affect expressors.

Your own facial expressions are probably characterized by one or another of these eight styles only to a minor extent. You may be an unwitting expressor of fear, but only when you are under stress. Or you may be a blanked expressor of anger, but only when dealing with authority figures. You may be a substitute expressor, but to such a slight degree that it is not evident to anyone. Everyone probably shows one of these styles some of the time or to a slight degree. For some people, however, one or another of these expressive styles may be quite pronounced; it strongly colors their facial expressions. If that is the case for you, it would be important that you know it, to be aware of how others may see your facial expressions. If you happen to be a flooded-affect expressor or a revealer, then you probably are already aware of it, and so is everyone who knows you, so there is no need to bring it to your attention. If you are characterized by one or more of the other six expressive styles, however, you may well not know it, and it is not easy to find out.

The ideal procedure would be to have videotapes made of your facial expressions in a number of live situations, and ask an expert in facial expression to study those videotapes and give you feedback. We will offer here a do-it-yourself alternative, recognizing that it may not work for everyone, or for every expressive style. (It won't spot the ever-ready expressor, which requires those real-life videotapes.) We do think it has a chance, and that you can learn enough in the process to justify the time you spend. Even if you do not have a pronounced style, you will learn about your own face, and more about how to recognize emotion in others.

There are three phases—taking pictures of your face, analyzing those pictures, and working with a mirror. You can do the last phase, the mirror work, without doing the first two and derive some benefit. But if you are going to do all three phases—and that is what we suggest you do—then you must not do the mirror work until last. Doing it before that will ruin your chance to learn about yourself from phases one and two.

phase 1: taking pictures

You need a set of fourteen still photographs of your face which meet the following criteria.

—They show your full face; the lighting is good; they are in focus; and they are all about the same size (jumbo size or larger).

—There are two pictures taken when you were feeling no emotion at all, two each when you were feeling surprise, fear, anger, disgust, sadness, and happiness.

—You were feeling just one of those emotions when each picture was taken, not a blend of two.

—You were not self-conscious or embarrassed about the photographs being taken; preferably you didn't know pictures were being taken.

It is unlikely you already have such a set of pictures. (If you do, skip to Phase 2, *Analyzing Pictures.*) The problem is how to approximate such a set of pictures. If you were taking a course in "Unmasking the Face," we would use role-playing situations in which you would follow a dramatic, involving plot line, reacting to what others do. Lacking that, we will outline some less desirable but still feasible techniques you can use. First, we will cover the mechanics, and then the procedures, for trying to experience the emotions.

You will need a partner to take pictures of you. Hopefully this will be someone with whom you can feel relaxed. The major stumbling block in this phase would be any feelings of embarrassment or foolishness about your facial expressions. Any camera that can take pictures at a distance of two-and-a-half feet or less will do, so that your face will occupy one-third or more of the picture. A Polaroid would be optimal, but a regular camera will do.

Have your partner set the camera on a tripod; or if you don't have a tripod, have him sit in a chair. Focus the camera so that you can get as close up as the camera will permit. Your partner should take all the pictures at a head-on angle, not from below or above, so that your full face is shown. The pictures can be taken indoors or outdoors, as long as the sun is not in your eyes. Use a chair or tripod to rest the camera on, and maintain the same distance through the series of photographs.

Cut out page 205 from the back of the book. It is a log sheet you will use in this phase and again in the next phase of analyzing the pictures. Because you will take more than one picture and will be experiencing more than one emotion, you must keep a log of what you were trying to do in each picture; this can be coordinated with the pictures themselves. If you are using a Polaroid camera, this will be easy, because you can write the number from your log sheet on the back of each picture as you go along. If you use a regular camera, but one in which the negatives come back in strips, it will be possible for you to figure out the order of the pictures and copy the log number on the back of each picture. If your camera or film processor cuts up the negatives, then you will have a problem figuring out which of the prints was made from which negative. You can avoid that problem by hanging an index card with a number written on it around your neck so you can readily coordinate the pictures with your log.

Before starting, work out a signal with your partner by which you can let him know at what instant you want him to take your picture. Raising the index finger is usually convenient; anything will do that doesn't require you to move your face. Get a clipboard and pencil, put your log on it, and you are now ready to go.

The first type of picture to take is fairly easy. Try to get a picture of your face when you are feeling completely neutral, not experiencing any emotion at all. It should be like the pictures of John and Patricia shown in Figures 5A and 13A. Look straight into the camera, try to think of nothing and to feel nothing. Try to relax, try to relax your face. When you feel you have achieved a neutral state, use your signal. Then write the word "neutral" next to number 1 on your log sheet, and also note how well you think you did. Take at least one more neutral picture. Each time write down your intention and how well you think you did. Stop when you have two pictures that you think, from your feelings on the inside, were neutral. It is important that you not use a mirror. We want your impression of how well you did to be based on what you usually must rely on—not looking in a mirror, but being aware of how it feels on the inside. For the same reason, if you are using a Polaroid, don't look at your pictures as you take them. Resist that temptation until you have finished. But have your partner write down the number of each picture on the back of the Polaroid prints. Also, don't have your partner encourage you, or comment on how well you are doing. When taking these neutral pictures and the ones of the emotions described below, it is important that your evaluations be based on your feeling, not your partner's opinion.

Now you should try to experience each of the emotions. There are a few ways to try, but it will take patience to succeed. The first technique is to close your eyes and try to remember as vividly as possible the most recent occasion on which you felt the particular emotion you are trying to capture. Or you can try to recall and relive the moment in your life when you felt that emotion most strongly. By either means, try to immerse yourself in that experience. Let yourself feel it inside, in your breathing, heartbeat, skin, in your facial expression.

When you are feeling it as much as you can—when the feeling has taken over —open your eyes; and when you feel certain you are showing it in your face, give your partner the signal to take your picture. After taking each picture, write next to the number on the log what you were trying to feel, and how well you think you succeeded in really feeling and showing it.

The procedure for experiencing the emotion may not work for all the emotions, or for any of them. It depends on you—how good you are at reliving experiences, how self-conscious you feel, how patient you are in trying, etc. With those emotions that you failed to experience, try to *imagine* what could happen in your life to make you feel them most intensely. Let your imagination go, and then try to put yourself in such an imaginary situation. Let the feeling come over you, feel it in your body and face.

If you can't remember any experience from the past, and you can't imagine any possible situation, you might try rereading the earlier chapters. Some people find that reading the "experience" section causes them to feel the emotion described. If that happens for you, try to go with it, and intensify the feelings. Or take one of the examples given in each chapter and see if that will work for you, but don't look at the figures in the chapters at this point.

If you have managed to take two pictures for each emotion in which you actually did feel it on the inside, and it felt as if it was showing in your face, then you can stop taking pictures. If you are still missing pictures for some or all the emotions, there is one more technique to try. Forget about experiencing, imagining, or otherwise creating the *feeling* and instead concentrate just on *posing* it in your face. Try to show the emotion in your face, concentrating on the feelings of your facial muscles. You may find that using this technique causes you to start feeling the emotion on the inside. If that happens, don't try to stop it. Allow yourself to feel the emotion as well as show it. Be sure with the posing procedure to obtain two pictures for each emotion in which you felt it was showing on your face.

At this point your log should show, next to each number, what you were trying and whether you felt you succeeded. Hopefully, by one of these techniques—reexperiencing, imagining, or posing—you have managed to get two pictures for each emotion. If you don't have pictures for one or two emotions, try again, or continue on to the next phase with what you have. If you have no pictures that you think were successful, then you are probably a withholder, or very self-conscious. In either case, the next phase won't be possible for you, and you should skip to the third phase, using the mirror.

phase 2: analyzing pictures

You have before you now a set of pictures. On the back of each picture you have written a number corresponding to your log. Now you need to recruit the help of at least three or four people, and preferably up to ten, who will act as judges of your pictures. It would be better if they were not your most intimate associates (no close relative), because they may know your idiosyncrasies, and at this point we are not after the idiosyncrasies. If you also took photographs of your partner, you can show the judges both sets of pictures. If you can get more than one judge to do the task at once, that is fine, as long as the judges don't compare their judgments until afterward.

Cut out the judgment sheet from the back of the book, page 206. Xerox as many copies of it as you will need, one for each judge for each person he judges. Sort through your stack of photographs. Eliminate those which your log says you were not able to show well, or at least pick the ones you thought you showed the best. Base this sorting on what your log says, *not* on what you think now that you look at the pictures. Shuffle the photographs you are going to show the judge. Give the judge a judgment sheet and his stack of shuffled photographs. Don't prompt or help him. Encourage him to make a judgment for each picture. He may find it hard with your neutral pictures because he doesn't have a choice of judging it as neutral, but try to get him to follow the instruction on the judgment sheet and make a guess whenever he is unsure. (The judges are not given a neutral choice because often people will use that choice whenever they are slightly uncertain, and because if given that choice it would not be possible to assess the possible presence of a frozen affect as described below.)

After you have at least three judges, you can tally the results. Get your log. On the far right side in the column labeled "Judgments," you can now write down the number of judges who called each of the pictures a particular emotion. For example, on a happy picture, you might be writing down that three out of four called it happy. If only one person called it surprise, you don't need to record that. If there is a real split with no very strong majority, then record on the log sheet all the judgments for each photograph, and how many judges made each judgment. Now you are ready to begin the analysis.

Take the *neutral* pictures you showed the judges and put them in front of you. Check what the log shows for these pictures:

1. The pictures were judged happy by most of the judges.
2. The pictures were judged sad by most of the judges.
3. The pictures were judged as either happy or sad by most of the judges.
4. There was little agreement; almost every emotion term was used by one or another judge.
5. At least one of the neutral pictures was judged as Surprise (or Fear, Anger, or Disgust) by half or more of the judges.

If your result was number 4, probably you don't have a frozen affect coloring your neutral facial expression, because there was no agreed-upon message.

Also, if your result was number 1, you probably don't have a frozen affect coloring your neutral facial expression, because "happy" is a frequent response that judges give to a neutral-looking face if they are forced to choose one of the emotion terms. Sad is also a frequent response to neutral faces, so if the result was 2 or 3, it is likely that you don't have a frozen affect coloring your neutral expression. Remember, the most extreme form of sadness results in a deadened, neutral-looking face. It is possible with result 2 or 3, however, that your neutral face might not have looked neutral or deadened, but might have shown some trace of the sadness blueprints. You can check on this by comparing your neutral faces with those shown in Chapter 9, comparing each area of the face separately. The best way to do this is to make three facial covers out of black paper. Cut one of them so that when you place it over one of your photographs only the brow and forehead show, another so that only the cheeks, nose, and mouth show, and a third so that only your eyes and lids show. Cover your neutral photograph so that only your brow/forehead shows. Compare it to Figure 51. Is it similar to that figure? If there is a resemblance, it will be slight. Don't expect to see in your picture anything as pronounced as in this figure. Now compare your eyes/lids with Figure 52 in the same manner, and your lower face with Figure 53. On the basis of these comparisons you should be able to determine whether you have a sadness frozen affect.

If the outcome of the judgments was number 5, that strongly suggests that whatever emotion was being judged in your face is often seen there. Remember, that could be because you are always maintaining some element of that emotion in your face rather than totally relaxing your face when you are not feeling any emotion (frozen affect). Or it could be a static signal, due simply to the particular construction of your face. For example, if you have deep-set eyes and a low eyebrow, people may judge you as angry. (Photograph 52 in the practice series described in Chapter 10 shows such an angry-looking neutral face caused by the construction of the face.) It is probably worth knowing that you tend to give that impression even when you are feeling neutral. If outcome 5 was your result, check each area of your photographs against the appropriate figures, using the facial covers over your neutral face, as we suggested above.

The next steps we will outline apply to each of the emotions you photographed. Lay out the photographs of an emotion in front of you. Check what the log says for each of those photographs.

1. The strong majority of the judges of both pictures named the emotion you were experiencing, imagining, or posing.
2. The majority of the judgments named the emotion you intended, but the rest of the judgments all, or almost all, named one other emotion; for

example, five out of ten judges called your surprise pictures Surprise, but three of the remaining five called them Fear.

3. There was almost an even split between the emotion you intended and one other emotion.
4. The majority of the judgments were of an emotion other than the one you intended.
5. There was no agreement among the judges about the emotion; no more than a third of the judges gave any one judgment.

If outcome 1 occurred for both of your pictures of a particular emotion, then there is no indication of any of the expressive styles.

If outcome 5 occurred for both of your pictures, and your log shows that you felt the emotion and thought you were showing it in your face, then it is likely that you are a blanked expressor for that emotion. You can't be certain, however. Perhaps you didn't show the emotion in your face because this picture-taking situation was too artificial. But there is a good likelihood you are a blanked expressor, and you may want to start checking on it. Suppose you found you were a blanked expressor for disgust. The next time you are in a situation when you are disgusted and think you are showing disgust, ask friends what you look like, whether they could tell how you felt, etc.

If outcome 5 occurs for all the emotions, or all except happiness, then it is likely you are a withholder. It is also possible that taking pictures of yourself just did not work for you. If you are a withholder, people who know you know that about you, so you should be able to check on it.

Outcomes 2, 3, and 4 all suggest a substitute expressor. Outcome 3 suggests this more than outcome 2, and outcome 4 more than 3. If one of these outcomes occurred for both of your pictures, and your log shows that you thought you had felt the emotion and were showing it, it is more likely you are a substitute expressor than if one of these outcomes occurred for only one of your pictures and on that picture you didn't record feeling the emotion or showing it very well. Suppose you are a disgust-for-anger substitute expressor. On your anger pictures, some of the judges (outcome 2), half (outcome 3), or most (outcome 4) might have judged you as disgusted. Use one of the facial covers to black out your "anger" pictures so that you can see only the lower face. Compare your lower facial expressions to the figures in the book for the lower face for anger and disgust. Can you see why the judges called you disgusted when you thought you showed anger? Do the same for the eyes/lids, and for the brows/forehead. In this way you can discover just what it is in your own facial expression that may have caused judges to see your face as disgusted when you thought you showed anger. This does not mean that you are not feeling anger, only that when you feel anger, people who see you may think you feel disgusted.

Of course, outcomes 2, 3, and 4 do not necessarily mean that you are a substitute expressor. The best way to check on this is again to photograph your face, trying again to experience the emotion for which you may be a substitute expressor. Pay particular attention to choosing an experience that does not call forth a blend of the emotion in question and the substitute emotion. Replace the other photographs of that emotion with the new ones and give the entire pack of pictures (not just the new ones) to other judges and see if this result occurs again. If it doesn't, you really can't be sure whether the first result or the second was correct. If, however, you find the same pattern of results again, then it is likely that you are a substitute expressor.

We have described ways for discovering, from the outcomes of the judgments of your photographs, whether you may be a withholder, blanked expressor, substitute expressor, or frozen-affect expressor. In the next phase we will describe different procedures that may be helpful in determining whether you are an unwitting expressor. These procedures are also relevant to assessing withholders, blanked expressors, and substitute expressors.

phase 3: using a mirror

In ordinary life you must rely upon feedback from your own facial muscles—the sensations that come internally from your face—both to know and to control your facial expressions. Good feedback from your face tells you when you are showing an emotion and what emotion you are showing (context, other sensations, memories, etc., can tell you this, too). It permits you to control your expression by qualifying it, masking it, or simulating an emotion when none is felt.

You can't constantly be asking people what your face looks like, and you can't arrange matters so you can see your face in a mirror while you are interacting. You should instead attend to feedback from your face. This feedback from your facial muscles may not be well-developed. You may have learned, for some reason, *not* to know how your face feels when you are showing a particular emotion, or all the emotions. If that is so, then look out for trouble. If you don't know how your face feels when the muscles are contracted in an angry expression, for example, then you may not know when you are showing that emotion (unwitting expressor). When you feel angry, you may be showing disgust instead (substitute expressor). Or you may be showing nothing on your face (blanked expressor). You may not be able to qualify your angry face. And you may be unable to simulate an angry look. Here, then, are some steps you can take to determine how well-acquainted you are with your own facial feedback.

You will need a hand mirror which you can hold easily, large enough to show you your entire face. And you will need to get over feeling self-conscious about making faces and looking at your own face. We will use anger as an example to explain the steps, but you can use the same steps for each emotion.

1. Turn to Figure 42 at the end of the anger chapter (for the other emotions, turn to the figure at the end of the appropriate chapter).
2. Try to imitate with your own face each picture in the figure.
3. Are you able to do it? Check in the mirror.
4. If you can't do it without looking in the mirror, look in the mirror while you try; imitate the faces in the figure.
5. If you are able to imitate them, note whether the feelings in your face are familiar, and whether it feels like anger. If it doesn't feel strange, but feels somehow right, follow the same procedure for the next emotion. If, however, you were unable to imitate the photographs in the figure while looking in the mirror or if you were able to duplicate the faces in the book but found the feeling strange and unfamilar, turn to Step 6.
6. Find the figure that shows just the brow/forehead position for the emotion; anger is the left photograph in Figure 31. Using the mirror, imitate that picture. If you can do it, ask yourself if it feels familiar or strange, and whether it feels like the emotion intended.
7. Turn to the figure for the eyes/lids, and do the same as in 6.
8. Turn to the figure for the lower face and do the same as in 6.
9. Try to hold one part of the face, let us say the brow/forehead, in the position shown in the book, and add another part of the face, and then the third. It doesn't matter which you start with. Can you make the total expression? Does it feel strange or familiar? Does it feel like the emotion intended?

If, in Step 5, you made the expression and it felt familiar and felt something like the emotion, then there is little likelihood that you are a withholder, a substitute expressor, a blanked expressor, or an unwitting expressor. If you didn't succeed in Step 5, but did reach that outcome by Step 9 (you were able to make the face, it felt familiar, and it felt something like the emotion), the same is true. If your only problem was in making the fear brow/forehead, or the sadness brow/forehead, but you were able to make the rest of the facial expression, then again the same would hold for you. The failure to make these two brows is probably due to some idiosyncrasy in your permanent facial structure. In general, as long as you are able to make the faces by either Step 5 or Step 9, utilizing two of the three facial areas, there is no evidence of one of these expressive styles.

If you could make the expression in Step 5 or 9 but it felt quite unfamiliar, then you may be an unwitting expressor of that emotion. You don't recognize what it feels like when you show an expression that others would recognize as that emotion. If in Step 5 or 9 you made the expression and it felt familiar, but felt like a different emotion than the intended one (for example, when successfully imitating the anger face, it felt like disgust), you may be a substitute expressor for this emotion.

What if you can't make the expression by Step 9? If you can't imitate either of the faces shown in the figure and your failure is not just in one facial area but in all three, then it is likely that you are a blanked expressor for that emotion. If you followed the procedures outlined in the first two phases, you should have learned that already. If you can't make the expression for most of the emotions, you are probably a withholder.

The steps in these three phases should teach you about your own face and increase your awareness of other people's facial expressions, even if they fail to reveal that you have any of the expressive styles outlined earlier. And, as we have said, if you do have one of these expressive styles, it is most likely to be slight, or only evident in some situations, or under stress, etc. If you have one of these expressive styles in a slight degree or only occasionally, then it won't be evident with the steps outlined in these three phases.

What if these steps suggest that you do have one of these expressive styles? And you believe, from following the steps outlined, that you achieved a pretty accurate reading of your face. Can you change it? Frankly, we don't know. We are just beginning to explore this question in our research. We are, however, optimistic. It may be that simply learning the blueprints of facial expression and practicing how to recognize them will diminish any of these expressive styles. Or the steps in these three phases may themselves reduce any expressive style. Or it may take special training on how to move the facial muscles. Certainly the more sensitive you become to the complexities of facial expression—the more you know about your own face—the richer will be your own emotional experience.

13

---

conclusion

In the previous chapters you have seen the blueprints of facial expression—how happiness, surprise, fear, anger, disgust, and sadness are registered in the face. You have also seen many of the blend expressions, in which two of these emotions are combined. Some of the ways people use facial expressions to punctuate their conversation, underlining a word or two, has also been shown, as have some of the other messages conveyed by the face. Reading this book and looking at the photographs should increase your understanding of facial expressions. If you did the extra work of making up faces and practicing with the flashing faces at the end of each chapter and the new faces described in Chapter 10, then you are more likely to have developed your understanding into a skill that will be part of you, something you can use without having to think about it. A further way to practice what you have learned about the appearance of the face is to watch people without hearing their words. By turning the sound off while watching television, you can do that without rudeness. A few hours of such practice can serve to heighten your awareness of facial expressions.

Reading the sections on the experience of the six emotions should help you better understand emotion, quite apart from what it looks like on the face. You can check the explanations of each emotion's dynamics against your own emotional experience to learn about your own feelings. For example, do you use all four routes to achieve happy feelings? Is one of the arousers of anger the most typical one for you? Which of the emotions do you dread the most? Which of the negative emotions do you enjoy?

The chapter on facial deceit explained why and how people control their facial expressions. Specific ways to recognize signs of control—modulating or falsifying expressions—were detailed. Clues to deceit, to picking up facial leakage, were also explained. Remember, you won't be able to use this information unless you have gone beyond understanding the photographs in the earlier chapters to acquire the skill in recognizing facial expression by making faces, flashing faces, and using the practice faces. The end of Chapter 11 explained what you must consider to determine whether or not someone is managing his face.

The last chapter was concerned with how you may use your own face. Eight different styles of facial expressions were described. Knowing about them may help you better understand others, and if you went through the steps outlined—photographing and analyzing your own face, following the techniques for using a mirror—then perhaps you uncovered some interesting facts about your own facial expressions.

Of course, knowing how someone feels or how you feel does not tell you what to do about it. You may not always be glad that you know how someone else feels, particularly if he didn't really want you to know it! Knowing how someone feels doesn't mean that you will necessarily want to do anything about it. For example, when someone is controlling his anger, and you now can spot that, if you acknowledge you know he is angry you may cause him to explode. Depending upon the situation, that may be either just what you don't want or what you do want. "Getting it all out" can be helpful or harmful, with any emotion. It depends upon you, the other person, the situation, your relationship, whether you both have an interest in sharing your feelings, etc. It may be that acknowledging another person's anger could be very helpful. He may not explode; instead he may now have the opportunity to tell you what is bothering him before it builds up.

We have written the book on an assumption underlying science and all intellectual activity—that to increase knowledge is useful. We believe this is so, and that to increase your knowledge of facial expressions and of the emotions will be useful. You will have to consider to what use you put that knowledge. But, useful or not, the subject itself compelled us to write this book. Faces are fascinating.

the facial blueprint photographs

A major challenge in writing this book was to find the best way to illustrate facial expressions. We knew we could not teach people practical information about facial expressions through words alone, that the key to this book would be showing the appearance of the face. In our research we had gathered thousands of photographs of facial expression and literally miles of motion-picture film and videotapes. We had facial expressions of normal persons, psychiatric patients, patients with brain damage; of children, young adults, and older people; of Americans and people from many other nations and cultures; of people talking in formal interviews, informally on the street or in their own turf, and in the "bush"; of spontaneous and posed expressions; of expressions taken when the person was unaware of being observed and of persons who took their own picture; of truthful, playful, phony, and deceitful faces. But we found we could not use this wealth of faces in this book.

To do more than just illustrate facial expressions, to show facial expressions in a way that would teach the reader skills in reading faces, we needed special pictures. The most important and difficult requirement to meet was to have pictures of the same person showing all the emotions. Only with such pictures would it be possible to hold constant the static and slow facial signals (which differ with any two people) and expose subtle differences in rapid facial signals by continually comparing pictures of the same person. Only with such pictures would it be possible to create composite photographs combining different pictures of the same person to visually demonstrate how each part of the face contributes to an emotion message. Other requirements were that the lighting always be the same, so that the contrast and detail would not vary; and that the full face be shown, so the features and wrinkles were not obscured by a camera angle. The last requirement was that the pictures be of people who would not be embarrassed by having their facial expressions exposed in this book.

Therefore, we specially made the pictures for this book, photographing faces under controlled laboratory conditions. Our two models followed detailed instructions based on the Facial Atlas. They were not told to feel an emotion, but rather were given instructions such as "lower your brow so that it looks like this," or "raise the outer corner of your upper lip," or "tighten your lower eyelid." The models recreated the faces we had seen and studied when people were really experiencing emotions. We were in a sense drawing with a camera—not relying on imagination, as an artist might, or on the models' possible dramatic skill in trying to feel an emotion, but tracing photographically the muscular movements shown in the Facial Atlas.

Expressions that are anatomically not possible, muscular movements that can be created in a drawing or a composite photograph but that can't happen in life, were excluded. Facial movements that have little to do with emotion—funny grimaces such as children make, or the variety of facial movements that signal something other than emotion, like a wink or sticking the tongue out, were also excluded. Facial movements that might occur when someone was experiencing an emotion but that were not unique to any one emotion or blend of emotions were also excluded. For example, people may bite their lower lip when they are afraid, angry, or sad. This movement was excluded because it can occur with three different emotions and therefore is not helpful in teaching the distinctions among emotions. Even when we excluded the anatomically impossible facial expressions, the expressions unrelated to emotion, and the expressions related to more than one emotion, there were still too many. Limiting ourselves just to those facial expressions which distinguish one emotion from another still involved so many pictures that the reader would be overwhelmed.

We decided to leave out the primitive forms of some of the emotional expressions—that is, the most extreme, least controlled versions of some of the emotions. These primitive expressions, which some scholars have said are the innate forms of emotions, are rarely shown except by an infant or young child, or by an adult under unusual and extreme duress. When they are seen they are readily understood. Their meaning is obvious and their message is almost always repeated in a simultaneous voice sound. Figure 61 is an example of the type of expression we have excluded—the primitive facial expression for the emotion of disgust. We have also excluded the primitive versions of sadness and happiness. We had to include the primtive expressions for surprise, fear, and anger in order to demonstrate certain key distinctions. But for the most part what we have shown are the facial expressions of emotion you are most likely to encounter in social life. Many are slight or mild

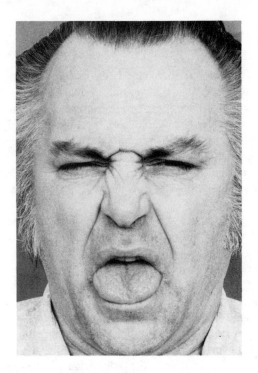

Figure 61

versions of the emotions. Some are controlled emotional expressions. Many show blends of two emotions. And there are some extreme emotional expressions that are seen less often, and usually in intimate situations.

Even when we had excluded some of the primitive expressions, there were still too many possible faces to show, for there are many ways each emotion can be registered on the face. There is not one face for each emotion, but a set or family of related but different expressions, often with each member of the set having a different but related nuance of meaning. For example, Chapter 5 shows a worried face, a controlled fear face, a slight fear face, a terror face, a shocked or startled fear face, an apprehensive fear face, and faces expressing fear-surprise, fear-sadness, fear-disgust, and fear-anger blends. These are different members of the fear family of faces.

Many of the variations in the facial expression for each emotion are due to differences in the lower face. The hinged jaw and the construction of the lips allows many different expressions in this part of the face. For some emotions there is also more than one expression in the eyelids or forehead. Some of these variations are the important ones, the *major* variants, which differ the most in appearance and meaning. With anger, for example, there are two major variants—the open, square-mouth anger and the closed, lip-press anger. These are included and discussed in Chapter 7.

Some of the *minor* variants have been excluded. For example, Figure 62 shows three anger mouths; 62A is one of the major variants, the closed lip-press; 62B and 62C are two minor variants on that mouth. These minor variants have been excluded both because their difference in appearance and meaning is not great and because the evidence about their specific nuance of meaning is not solid. The mouth in 62B probably indicates frustration or resignation in addition to the major theme of controlled anger. In 62C the forward pursed lip-press probably indicates a more "schoolmarm" type of anger.

Patricia and John are the two models whose faces appeared in chapters 4 through 9. We wanted both a male and a female so you could see how emotions appear regardless of the person's sex. We wanted two people who differ in the amount of permanent wrinkles (John is eleven years older than Patricia) and in facial features (compare the size and shape of their eyes). Patricia and John were both skilled in moving their facial muscles on command, were willing to do so and to have their faces made public. John has just finished his doctoral training with the authors; in the course of his work as a student, he has spent years practicing with a mirror to learn control of his facial muscles. Patricia, an artist, is married to one of the authors and, by coincidence, talent, or fate, knew without ever practicing how to control her facial muscles.

Figure 62

A

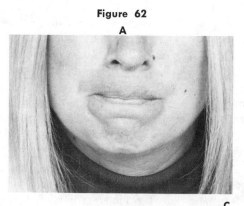

B   C

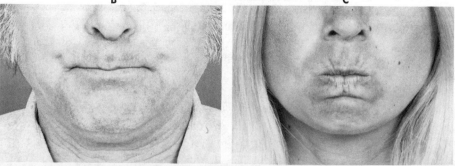

practice photos
for chapter 10

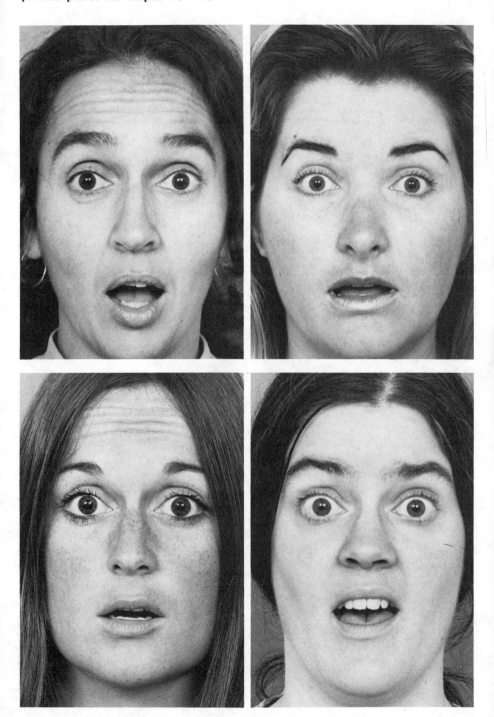

2

1

4

3

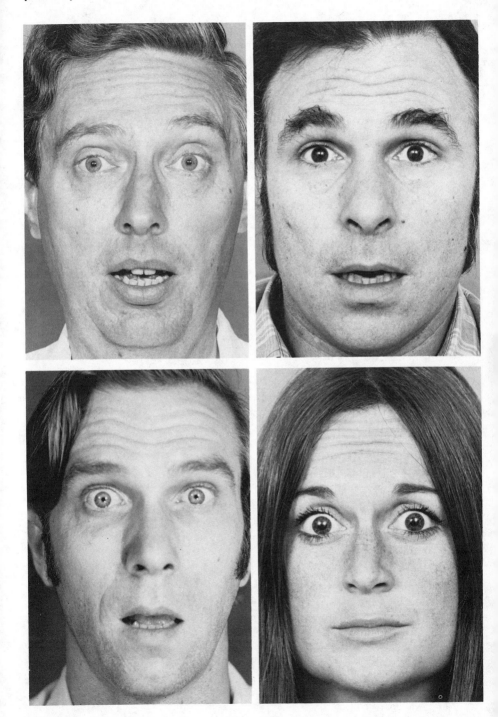

6

5

8

7

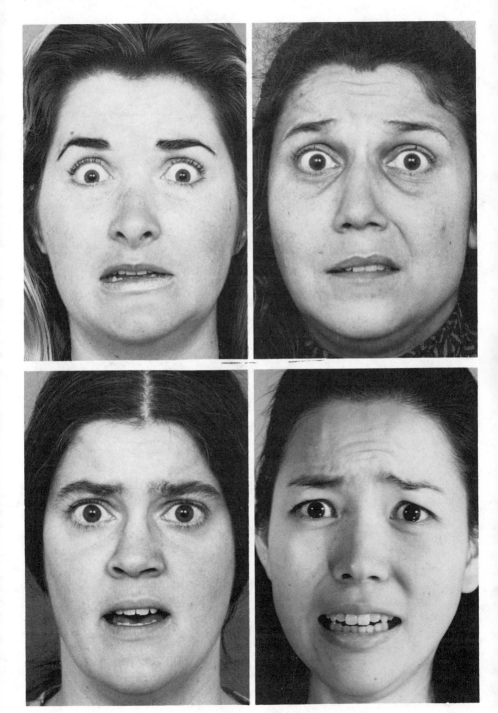

10

9

12

11

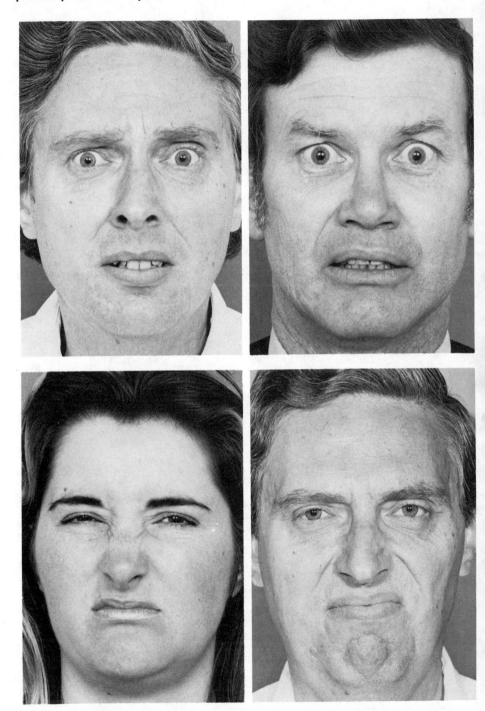

14

13

16

15

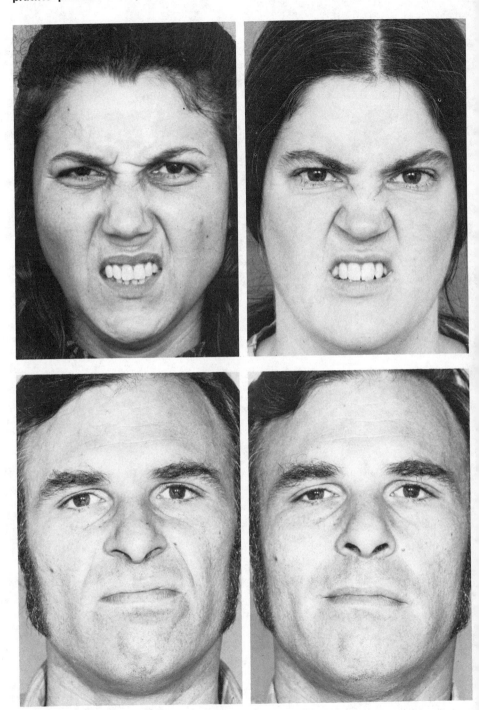

18

17

20

19

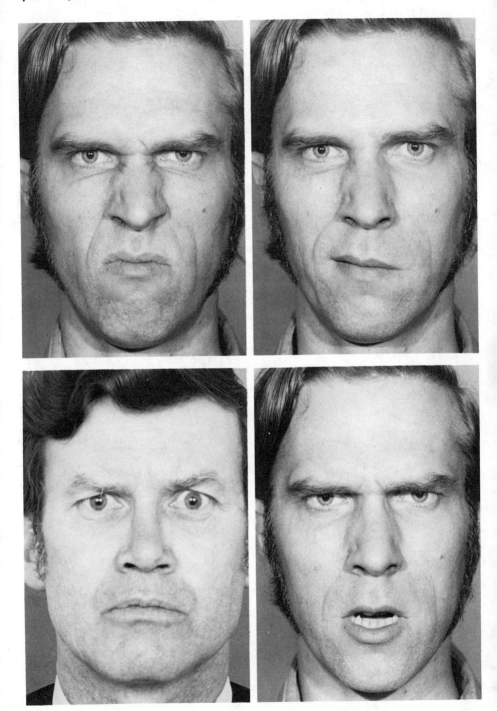

22

21

24

23

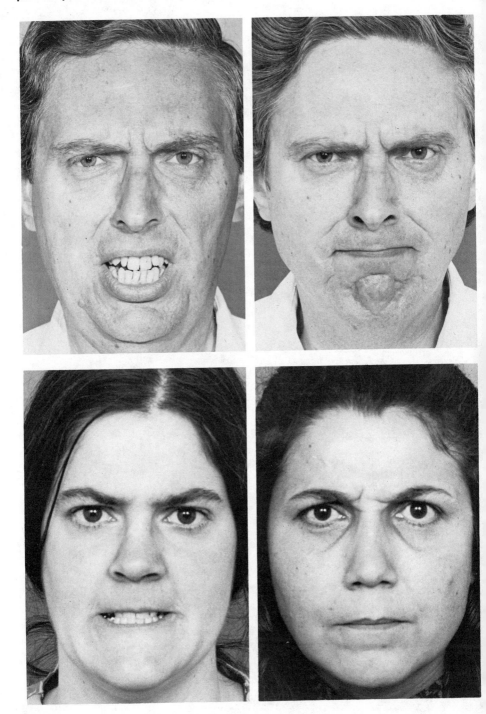

26

25

28

27

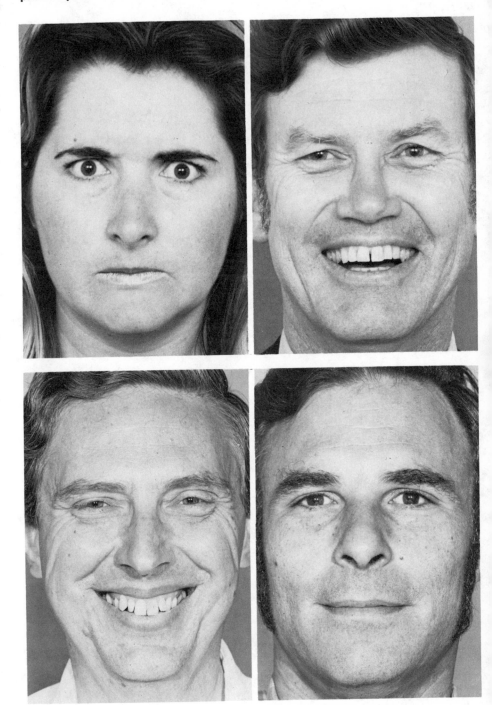

30

29

32

31

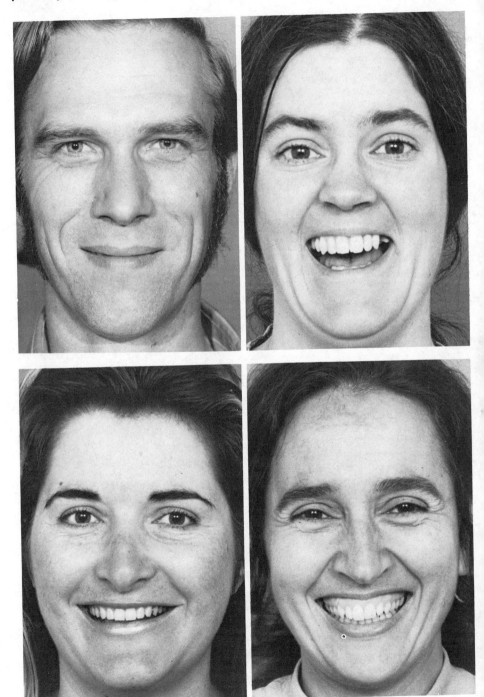

34

33

36

35

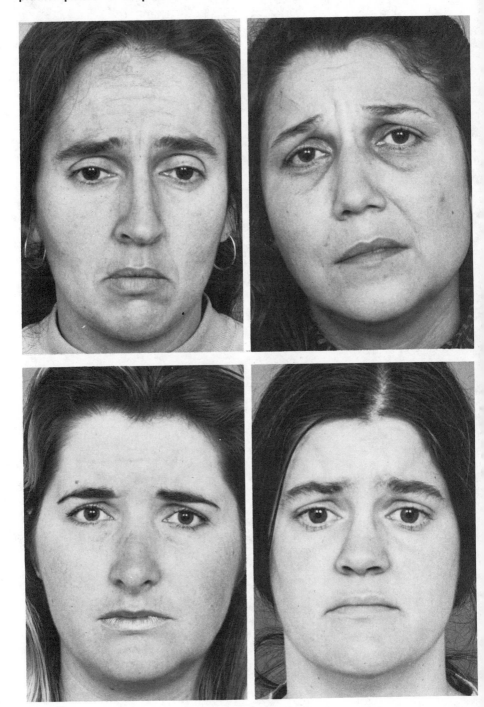

38

37

40

39

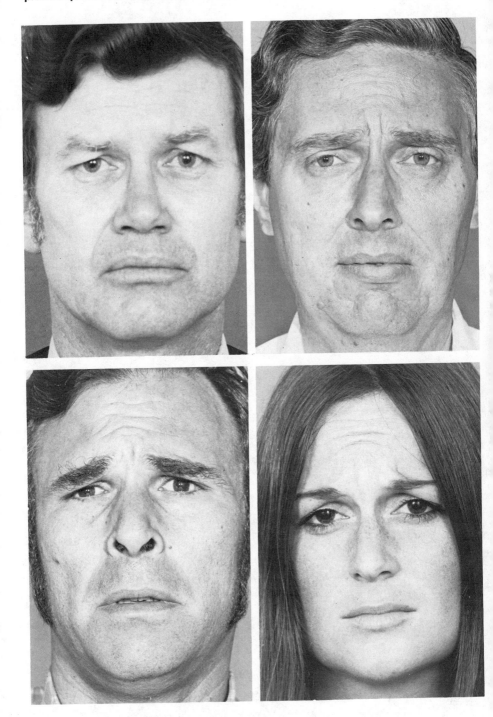

42

41

44

43

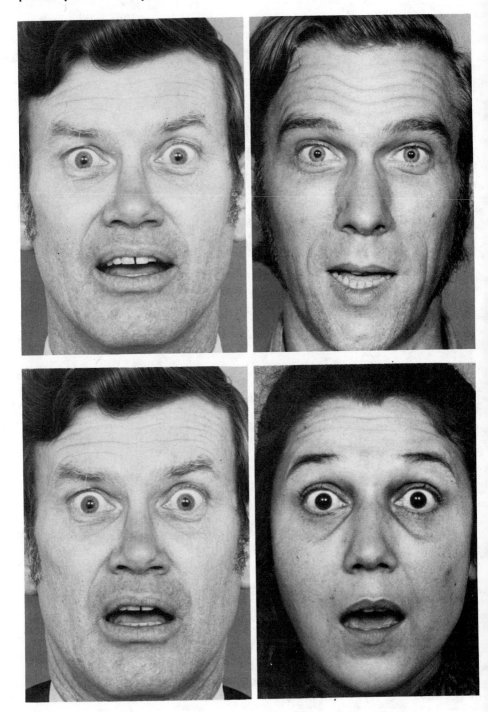

46

45

48

47

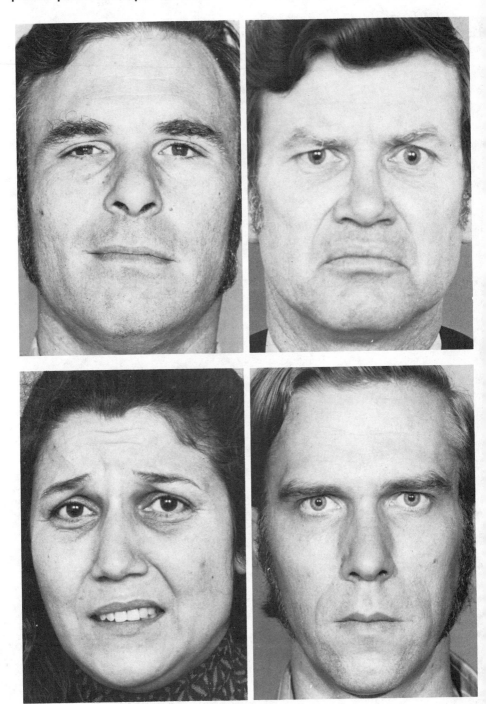

50

49

52

51

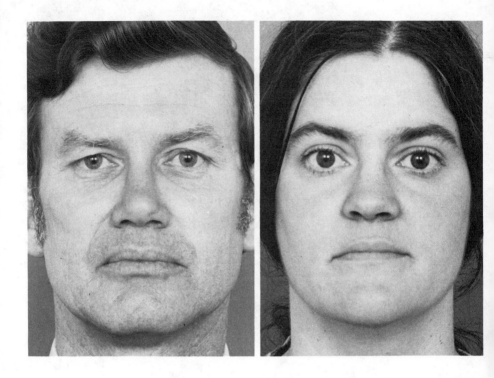

54   53

log and judge sheets

Judgment Sheet for Practice Photos
(See p. 129 of Chapter 10)

PHOTO #	BLINK-JUDGMENT	SECOND JUDGMENT

Log for Photographing Your Own Facial Expressions

You should try to take at least two pictures of yourself for each of the following expressions: Neutral, Happy, Sad, Fear, Disgust, Anger, and Surprise.

PHOTO #	INTENDED EMOTION	HOW WELL YOU EXPRESSED IT	JUDGMENTS (Fill in later. See page 161)
1.			
2.			
3.			
4.			
5.			
6.			
7.			
8.			
9.			
10.			
11.			
12.			
13.			
14.			
15.			
16.			
17.			
18.			
19.			
20.			

Judgment Sheet

Circle one word for each picture you see. Write the number from the back of the picture in the space provided. Even if you are not sure of your answer, make a guess for every picture. Do not spend too much time on any one answer; your first impression is usually best.

PHOTO #

	HAPPY	SAD	FEAR	ANGER	SURPRISE	DISGUST
	HAPPY	SAD	FEAR	ANGER	SURPRISE	DISGUST
	HAPPY	SAD	FEAR	ANGER	SURPRISE	DISGUST
	HAPPY	SAD	FEAR	ANGER	SURPRISE	DISGUST
	HAPPY	SAD	FEAR	ANGER	SURPRISE	DISGUST
	HAPPY	SAD	FEAR	ANGER	SURPRISE	DISGUST
	HAPPY	SAD	FEAR	ANGER	SURPRISE	DISGUST
	HAPPY	SAD	FEAR	ANGER	SURPRISE	DISGUST
	HAPPY	SAD	FEAR	ANGER	SURPRISE	DISGUST
	HAPPY	SAD	FEAR	ANGER	SURPRISE	DISGUST
	HAPPY	SAD	FEAR	ANGER	SURPRISE	DISGUST
	HAPPY	SAD	FEAR	ANGER	SURPRISE	DISGUST
	HAPPY	SAD	FEAR	ANGER	SURPRISE	DISGUST
	HAPPY	SAD	FEAR	ANGER	SURPRISE	DISGUST

Pictures of Facial Affect

Many of the photographs in this book are available as a set of 110 35-mm slide transparencies, plastic mounted. These black and white photographs show 14 human faces expressing six emotions: fear, anger, happiness, sadness, surprise, and disgust. They are useful for research and for training psychologists, psychiatrists, actors, and others. (For a four-page description of the set and ordering information, send a stamped, self-addressed envelope to "PFA", c/o CPP, Inc., P.O. Box 60070, Palo Alto, CA 94306.)

Facial Action Coding System

The methods for measuring and scoring facial behavior mentioned on pages 28*ff.* are described in a complete self-instructional atlas that identifies "action units" and provides illustrative photographs, film strips, practice materials, and a 16-mm training film. To investigate this sophisticated research technique, send $7.50 for the *Investigator's Guide to FACS* (item #6701) to CPP, Inc., P.O. Box 60070, Palo Alto, CA 94306.

index

A

Accuracy, in judging facial expressions, 22-23
Actors, 4
Anger, 1, 12, 14, 78-98
  ambiguity of, 88-89
  appearance of, 82-98
  brow, 82-83
  –disgust blends, 67-68, 76, 81, 92-94
  display rules, 138
  experience of, 78-82
  eyes, 83
  Facial Atlas and, 28-31
  –fear blends, 79, 81, 94-95
  flashing faces, 98
  –happiness blends, 81, 95, 102, 107, 110
  intensity of, 92
  leakage and deception clues, 148-49
  making faces, 97-98
  mouth, 83-88
  –sadness blends, 81, 95, 115-16, 122-25
  simulating, 148-49
  –surprise blends, 81, 94
Appearance:
  of anger, 82-98
  of disgust, 68-77
  of fear, 50-65
  of happiness, 103-13
  of sadness, 116-28
  of surprise, 37-46
Apprehension, 49, 55, 83

B

Blanked expressors, 155-56, 163-66

Body movement, 7, 17, 18, 151, 152
Brow:
  anger, 82-83
  disgust, 69
  fear, 50-52
  happiness, 103, 107
  sadness, 117-19
  surprise, 37-39

C

Contempt, 67, 68, 71, 79
  –happiness blends, 102, 107
Controlling facial expressions, 19-20, 31-32, 137-40
Conversations, 15-18
Cosmetics, 11
Cultural display rules, 137-38, 143, 154, 155
Customers, 4

D

Darwin, Charles, 23, 27, 28, 32, 80, 114
Darwin and Facial Expression (Ekman and Friesen), 6
Deception clues, 144-45
  location, 145, 151
  micro-expressions, 145, 151-52
  morphology, 145-50
  timing, 145, 150-51
Disgust, 1, 13, 14, 66-77
  –anger blends, 67-68, 76, 81, 92-94
  appearance of, 68-77
  brow, 69
  contempt expressions, 71

Disgust *(cont.)*
  experience of, 66-68
  eyes, 68, 69
  Facial Atlas and, 28-31
  –fear blends, 68, 74-75
  flashing faces, 98
  –happiness blends, 68, 76, 102
  heart-rate acceleration and decelera-
    tion, 30
  leakage and deception clues, 149
  lower face, 68-71
  making faces, 77
  –sadness blends, 68, 76, 116, 125
  simulating, 149
  –surprise blends, 68, 71-74
  variations in intensity, 71
Display rules, 24, 137-39
  cultural, 137-38, 143, 154, 155
  personal, 139, 154
Distress, 48, 114-16
Duchenne, Guillaume, 28

E

Eibl-Eibesfeldt, Iraneus, 27
Emblems, 12-14, 39, 40, 42, 69, 147,
  149
Emotion in the Human Face (Ekman
  and Friesen), 6
Emotions *(see also* Anger; Disgust;
    Fear; Happiness; Sadness; Sur-
    prise)
  defined, 11
Ever-ready expressors, 156
Excitement, 99-100
Experience:
  of anger, 78-82
  of disgust, 66-68
  of fear, 47-50
  of happiness, 99-102
  of sadness, 114-16
  of surprise, 34-37
Eyebrow-flash, 39
Eyes:
  anger, 83
  disgust, 68, 69
  fear, 52-53
  happiness, 105-7
  sadness, 119
  surprise, 40

F

Facial Atlas, 28-31, 170
Facial deceit, 32, 102, 135-53
  leakage and deception clues, sources
    of, 145-52
  management techniques, 140-43
  obstacles to recognizing, 143-45
  reasons for controlling expressions,
    137-40
Facial emblems *(see* Emblems)
Facial expressions of emotion:
  accuracy of judgements of, 22-23
  analyzing pictures of, 160-64
  blanked expressors, 155-56, 163-66
  checking your own, 154-66
  controlling, 19-20, 31-32, 137-40
  deception clues, 144-52
  ever-ready expressors, 156
  Facial Atlas, 28-31, 170
  falsifying, 141-43, 144, 146
  flooded-effect expressors, 157
  frozen-effect expressors, 156
  leakage, 31, 144-52
  location in conversation, 145, 151
  management techniques, 140-43
  masking, 142-43
  micro-expressions, 14-15, 145, 151-
    52
  mirror, use of, 164-66
  modulating, 141, 144, 146
  morphology, 145-50
  neutralizing, 142, 144
  obstacles to recognizing management
    of, 143-45
  qualifying, 140-41, 143-44
  research on, 21-33
  revealers, 155
  simulating, 141-43
  styles of, 155-57
  substitute expressors, 2, 156, 163-65
  taking pictures of, 158-60
  timing, 145, 150-51
  universality of, 23-28
  unwitting expressors, 1-2, 155, 164-
    66
  withholders, 1, 155, 163-66
Facial leakage *(see* Leakage)
Facial management techniques, 140-43
  falsifying, 141-43, 144, 146
  modulating, 141, 144, 146

Facial management techniques (*cont.*)
  obstacles to recognizing, 143-45
  qualifying, 140-41, 143-44
Facial punctuators (*see* Punctuators)
Facial signals:
  rapid, 11-13, 14, 169
  slow, 11, 14, 169
  static, 10-11, 14, 154, 169
Falsifying facial expressions, 141-43,
    144, 146
Fear, 1, 3, 14, 19-20, 47-65
  –anger blends, 79, 81, 94-85
  appearance of, 50-65
  brow, 50-52
  differentiated from surprise, 48-49
  –disgust blends, 68, 74-75
  experience of, 47-50
  eye, 52-53
  Facial Atlas and, 28-31
  flashing faces, 63-64
  –happiness blends, 102, 110-11
  intensity of, 55
  leakage and deception clues, 148
  making faces, 63-64
  masking, 147-48
  modulating, 141
  mouth, 53-55
  –sadness blends, 116, 122
  simulating, 148
  startle reaction, 36-37, 48
  –surprise blends, 36, 60-62
  two-way expressions, 55-60
Flooded-affect expressor, 157
Frozen-affect expressors, 156
Frustration, 78-79

H

Hair styles, 11
Hand/arm movements, 17, 18
Happiness, 1, 14, 99-113
  –anger blends, 81, 95, 102, 107, 110
  appearance of, 103-13
  brow, 103, 107
  –contempt blends, 102, 107
  –disgust blends, 68, 76, 102
  experience of, 99-102
  eyes, 105-7
  Facial Atlas and, 28-31
  –fear blends, 102, 110-11

Happiness (*cont.*)
  flashing faces, 127-28
  intensity, 103-7
  leakage and deception clues, 147
  making faces, 112-13
  mouth, 103-5
  –sadness blends, 102, 116, 125-26
  simulating, 147
  –surprise blends, 102, 107
Heider, Eleanor, 26, 27
Heider, Karl, 26, 27
Henry V (Shakespeare), 80
Hjortsjö, Carl-Herman, 30-31
Huber, Ernst, 28

I

Intensity:
  of anger, 92
  of disgust, 71
  of fear, 55
  of happiness, 103-7
  of sadness, 121-22
  of surprise, 42-43
Izard, Carroll, 26, 27

J

Job applicants, 4
Jurymen, 4

L

Leakage, 31, 144-45
  location, 145, 151
  micro-expressions, 145, 151-52
  morphology, 145-50
  timing, 145, 150-51
Leg/feet movements, 17, 18
Listening, 17-18
Loan seekers, 4
Location of facial expressions, 145, 151
Lower face (*see also* Mouth)
  disgust, 68-71
  surprise, 40-42

M

Masking, 142-43, 147-48

Micro-expressions, 14-15, 145, 151-52
Ministers, 3
Mirror, use of, 164-66
Mock expressions, 14, 42, 70
Modulating facial expressions, 141, 144, 146
Moods, defined, 12
Morphology, leakage and deception clues and, 145-50
Mouth (*see also* Lower face)
  anger, 83-88
  fear, 53-55
  happiness, 103-5
  sadness, 119-21

N

Neutralizing facial expressions, 142, 144
Nurses, 3

P

Pain, 47-48
Personal display rules, 139, 154
Personnel managers, 3
Physicians, 3
Pleasure, 99, 100
Plutchik, Robert, 28
Practice faces, 129-34
Psychotherapists, 3
Punctuators, 13, 14, 39, 40, 42, 70, 147, 150

Q

Qualifying facial expressions, 140-41, 143-44

R

Rapid facial signals, 11-13, 14, 169
Revealers, 155

S

Sadism, 81

Sadness, 1, 3, 14, 114-28
  –anger blends, 81, 95, 115–16, 122-25
  appearance of, 116-28
  brow, 117-19
  –disgust blends, 68, 76, 116, 125
  display rules, 138
  experience of, 114-16
  eyes, 119
  Facial Atlas and, 28-31
  –fear blends, 116, 122
  flashing faces, 127-28
  full-face, 121-22
  –happiness blends, 102, 116, 125-26
  intensity, 121-22
  leakage and deception clues, 149-50
  making faces, 126-27
  mouth, 119-21
  simulating, 149-50
Salesmen, 3
Self-concept, 101
Sexual experiences, 100, 102
Shakespeare, William, 80
Simulation, 141-43
  of anger, 148-49
  of disgust, 149
  of fear, 148
  of happiness, 147
  of sadness, 149-50
  of surprise, 147
Slow facial signals, 11, 14, 169
Smile, 101-5, 140, 142-43
Startle reaction, 36-37, 48
Static facial signals, 10-11, 14, 154, 169
Substitute expressors, 2, 156, 163-65
Surprise, 1, 13, 14, 34-46
  –anger blends, 81, 94
  appearance of, 37-46
  brow, 37-39
  differentiated from fear, 48-49
  –disgust blends, 68, 71-74
  experience of, 34-37
  eyes, 40
  Facial Atlas and, 28-31
  –fear blends, 36, 60-62
  flashing faces, 63-64
  –happiness blends, 102, 107
  heart-rate acceleration and deceleration, 30
  intensity, 42-43

Surprise (*cont.*)
  leakage and deception clues, 147
  lower face, 40-42
  making faces, 45-46
  masking, 147-48
  simulating, 147
  startle reaction, 36-37, 48
  types of, 43

T

Teachers, 3-4
Terror, 48, 49, 55
Timing of facial expressions, 145, 150-51
Tomkins, Silvan, 28, 32, 99
Trial lawyers, 3

U

Universality of facial expressions, 23-28
Unwitting expressors, 102, 155, 164-66

V

Voice, 17, 18, 152
Voters, 4

W

Withholders, 1, 155, 163-66
Words, 17, 18, 135-36